The Beginnings of
School Readiness

The Beginnings of School Readiness

Foundations of the Infant and Toddler Classroom

Sarah Taylor Vanover

ROWMAN & LITTLEFIELD
Lanham • Boulder • New York • London

Published by Rowman & Littlefield
A wholly owned subsidiary of The Rowman & Littlefield Publishing Group, Inc.
4501 Forbes Boulevard, Suite 200, Lanham, Maryland 20706
www.rowman.com

Unit A, Whitacre Mews, 26-34 Stannary Street, London SE11 4AB, United Kingdom

Copyright © 2017 by Sarah Taylor Vanover

All rights reserved. No part of this book may be reproduced in any form or by any electronic or mechanical means, including information storage and retrieval systems, without written permission from the publisher, except by a reviewer who may quote passages in a review.

British Library Cataloguing in Publication Information Available

Library of Congress Cataloging-in-Publication Data

Includes bibliographic references.

ISBN: 978-1-4758-3587-8 (cloth : alk. paper)
ISBN: 978-1-4758-3588-5 (pbk. : alk. paper)
ISBN: 978-1-4758-3589-5 (electronic)

∞™ The paper used in this publication meets the minimum requirements of American National Standard for Information Sciences—Permanence of Paper for Printed Library Materials, ANSI/NISO Z39.48-1992.

Printed in the United States of America

This book is dedicated to my husband, Rob, who read each and every draft and supported me every step of the way!

Contents

Introduction		ix
1	Social and Emotional Skills	1
2	The Importance of Routines	11
3	Infant and Toddler Language Skills	19
4	Promoting Play Skills	31
5	Physical Development of Infants and Toddlers	43
6	Developing Self-Help Skills	55
7	Cognitive Development and Pre-Academic Skills	67
8	Assessment and Early Intervention	77
9	Parent Involvement in the Infant-Toddler Classrooms	87
References		99
About the Author		103

Introduction

"School readiness" has become a popular term for preparing each young child to be successful in kindergarten. With increased elementary school standards and teacher accountability, kindergarten expectations have become rigorous. Children spend much of their day sitting in seats while working on early reading and math skills. There has been a huge shift from the play-based learning environment seen a generation or two in the past to beginning a traditional elementary education with five-year-old students.

Although many kindergarten classrooms begin by teaching alphabet letters at the beginning of the school year, by winter break, students are focused on reading short words. Young students are required to follow directions, focus on the teacher's lessons, and demonstrate self-control. Physical activity during the school day is limited due to large academic demands.

As families look ahead to these daunting academic standards, they are often tempted to begin teaching their children these academic skills at a young age. Families who place their children in childcare programs frequently ask the preschool classrooms to focus more on the academic piece of school readiness; however, that is only one portion of the skills needed to be prepared for kindergarten.

When you ask kindergarten teachers, they will frequently tell you that they have been trained to teach children the alphabet and how to read. That is part of the yearly curriculum that they plan for their students. When students arrive at kindergarten without well-developed social skills, the ability to follow instructions, or the ability to zip their own coats, the kindergarten teachers must stop their academic curriculum to address other skills.

By this standard, school readiness means more than a young child who can identify letters and numbers. It means more than a young child who is prepared to learn to read. School readiness addresses skills in all of the developmental (e.g., motor, language, cognition, social, and emotional areas skills). Families and early childhood educators need to view school readiness with regard to preparing the whole child for the next stage of life in elementary school.

DEFINING "SCHOOL READINESS"

"School readiness" can be defined as each child beginning school with the skills that he or she needs in order to benefit, to learn, and to be successful. Many early childhood specialists believe that school readiness goes far beyond the abilities of the children. Children are strongly influenced by those in their natural environment like family members, friends, teachers, and members of the community, so it is essential that each child's community encourages learning and support (Maxwell and Clifford, 2004).

The families and childcare programs must work together to create an environment that gives the student confidence to try new things and learn from past mistakes. Relationships are the foundation for additional learning. The teachers and caregivers must determine how each child learns (i.e., visually, kinesthetically) and find learning strategies for that student to be successful. It is also essential for the first few years of learning to be positive experiences so that children develop a thirst for knowledge. When we look at the areas of school readiness and the skills that children need to enter school, they can be divided into five categories:

1. Health and physical growth
2. Language and communication skills
3. Social and emotional skills
4. Independence and disposition skills
5. Cognitive and academic skills

AREAS OF SCHOOL READINESS

Using five broad categories for school readiness skills seems very vague until you analyze the skills in each category. Led by Pamela High (2008), the American Academy of Pediatrics created a summary of these categories. They described health and physical skills to include health status, growth, and disability. Social and emotional skills include turn-taking, cooperation, empathy, and the ability to express one's own emotions. Independence and disposition skills include self-help skills like feeding, diapering, and dressing, along with enthusiasm, curiosity, temperament, culture, and values. Language and communication skills include listening, speaking, and vocabulary, as well as literacy skills like print awareness, story sense, and writing and drawing processes. Cognitive skills include problem-solving, sound-letter association, spatial relations, and number concepts. A summative list of school readiness skills would look like this:

Health and physical growth
- eats a balanced diet
- gets plenty of rest
- receives all required immunizations and medical exams
- runs, jumps, climbs, and does other activities that develop large muscles
- uses pencils, crayons, scissors, paints, and other small motor activities

Language and communication skills
- will speak with children or adults
- speaks in five-word or six-word sentences
- takes turns in a conversation
- sings simple songs
- knows full name
- reads and writes own name
- can recite home address, phone number, and birthday
- knows how a book works
- recognizes familiar print from surroundings (logos, traffic signs, etc.)
- listens and responds to stories read to them
- uses scribbles and drawings to express ideas
- recites the letters of the alphabet

Social and emotional skills
- plays and shares with other children
- follows simple rules and routines
- demonstrates pretend play
- expresses own needs and wants
- explores and tries new things
- separates easily from parents and family
- works well alone
- is able to focus on one activity until it is complete
- asks for help when encountering a problem

Independence and disposition skills
- uses the toilet without help
- fastens and unfastens clothing without help (zippers, snaps, Velcro)
- feeds oneself using utensils
- helps put away toys or clothing
- keeps track of personal belongings
- covers mouth or nose when sneezing or coughing
- is enthusiastic about learning new things

- is curious about the world around him
- can express values that are important to oneself and the family

Cognitive and academic skills
- sorts and classifies objects
- knows same and different
- identifies basic colors
- counts in a sequence (rote counting) up to thirty
- counts sets of objects up to ten
- matches the printed number with objects up to ten
- recognizes, identifies, and copies basic shapes
- asks questions such as who, what, when, where, how, and why
- understands simple concepts of time (night and day, today, yesterday, and tomorrow)

Although there are many skills listed, only a portion of these school readiness skills are academic. Many of them have to do with the children's social and emotional skills, along with the other domains of learning.

School readiness also requires children to access learning opportunities. When families do not have access to basic necessities like housing, food, or warm clothing, it is extremely difficult for a young child to focus on learning. At the same time, all children need a safe learning environment with caregivers they trust. High-quality early childhood education should be accessible to all young children in order to help them prepare for kindergarten.

If it is obvious that a young child is falling behind developmentally, it is essential for the early childhood education specialist or the pediatrician to recommend early intervention services. If a child is not crawling or walking in the normal developmental window, then the caregiver or the pediatrician can recommend physical therapy. The physical therapist can work with the child and the family to increase the child's large muscle skills. These services are most successful when every member of the child's support team (the family, the caregivers, the doctor, and the therapists) work together to create a more comprehensive approach to service. Children who fall behind and do not receive this type of support services are more likely to fall further behind once they begin elementary school. The sooner help is offered, the larger the chance of helping the child achieve typical development.

ARE SCHOOLS READY FOR CHILDREN?

As families and early childhood educators push young children to be prepared to start school, there is also cause to step back and examine if the schools are ready for the children. The families and preschool programs can help children learn independence skills and to identify letters, but with such a large life transition at the age of five years, quality elementary schools should be preparing to accept these students into the next stage of their education. Elementary schools also need to anticipate an adjustment period for young students as they assimilate into a new environment.

This transition process should begin well before a child even registers for kindergarten. The elementary schools need to initiate partnerships with the early childhood education programs in order to collaborate with one another on curriculum and classroom expectations. These two programs also need to share resources for families in need of additional support like housing, food, or intervention for children with disabilities. When children are preparing to register for kindergarten, the elementary schools need to ease this transition by explaining to early childhood programs how families can register a child, prepare an Individualized Education Plan for students in the elementary school, and communicate kindergarten expectations to new families.

It is essential for elementary schools to serve the children in their communities and anticipate that children entering kindergarten will arrive to school at many different levels of development. Even though students in older classrooms are equipped to sit at desks for longer periods of time, it is critical for teachers to allow kindergarten students to move around the classroom more and use hands-on tools for learning.

In order to help new kindergarten students be successful, the curriculum in the classroom must build on the students' prior knowledge. Children arrive at school with their own set of skills and knowledge and will view their learning experiences through those experiences. If a child associates the fire alarm with the house fire that his family had two years ago, then his first fire drill in elementary school could be very alarming. When a teacher plans a new activity, then he or she should incorporate previous knowledge into that skill. For example, many children would not have sat in desks before kindergarten, so the teacher may initially want to teach rote counting (counting in sequence) by counting the number of jumping jacks the students can do instead of counting on a number line.

It is also critical for schools to remember that each new kindergarten student is affected by his culture and his language skills. If a student is not proficient at speaking English, then he may have difficulty in all areas of the classroom. If a student's cultural customs are different from those represented in the classroom, then she may demonstrate the rules that she already understands instead of new rules. For example, if a parent is still dressing the child at home and putting her coat on each morning, then she may not understand that her classroom requires more independence. The elementary school needs to be sensitive to the needs of the student, but the teachers must assist her with demonstrating the expected behaviors and responsibilities during the school day.

Finally, to encourage growth and development in young kindergarten students, the teachers must have a strong knowledge of child development. Elementary schools are often required to assess children on skills that are not developmentally appropriate for the children. The schools implement these tests and expectations because they are held accountable to the district, the state, and the federal Department of Education for showing continued improvement in student skills.

Teachers who work with young students each day need to be well aware of what the students are capable of doing and when the students need a break from structured and rigorous activity. It is also important for kindergarten teachers to know the child development milestones so that they can identify when the children in the class are not meeting these goals and offer those children extra support.

STEPPING BACK TO THE INFANT AND TODDLER CLASSROOMS

Looking at kindergarten expectations can be very overwhelming, and when preschool teachers create a list of the skills their students must have to be successful in kindergarten, it can be overwhelming to attempt to have every preschool student prepared for kindergarten in a year, or even two years, of preschool. John Bowlby, a British psychoanalyst, came up with the concept of "sensitive periods" when he was studying child development (Berk, 2012). He believed that there are certain windows in a child's development when the child is more adept at learning developmental skills. For example, he believed that an infant is much more adept at learning social skills starting at birth.

The baby desires to be close to the mother and learns to respond by cooing, babbling, and smiling. If the infant did not have the opportunity to create social relationships until preschool, it would be much harder to teach these skills. The infant's instinct desires to learn at a younger age, and once the child is three years old, she should be learning how to interact with other children instead of making initial social contacts.

The sensitive period for language skills also begins long before preschool starts. Research has shown that babies who hear more words and take more "conversational" turns during infancy develop stronger language skills as two-year-olds (Gilkerson and Richards, 2009). If infants and toddlers can absorb these key developmental skills, then it seems natural to conclude that many foundational skills needed for kindergarten begin when a child is in the infant or toddler classroom, not in preschool. Infants and toddlers may not be reading yet, but they are forming secure relationships, learning language, exploring their classroom environment, learning self-help skills like feeding and self-soothing, and playing in a group setting.

High-quality infant and toddler classrooms offer young children all of these opportunities: to create secure relationships with caregivers, to explore the classroom environment, to begin accomplishing individual goals like self-feeding, and to interact with same-age peers. This does not mean that every infant and toddler in childcare has the same learning opportunities. Children who spend their time in cribs or strapped into swings all day without a responsive caregiver and opportunities to explore will miss their opportunities to take advantage of the sensitive periods and maximize learning. This is why it is essential that all infant and toddler classrooms have trained caregivers who know how to create loving and child-friendly environments. It is also essential that adults, caregivers, and families understand the importance of the infant and toddler classrooms.

CHILDCARE PROVIDERS VALUING THE INFANT-TODDLER CLASSROOM

Just like it is important for kindergarten teachers to understand a young child's development to ensure school readiness, it is also critical that infant and toddler caregivers understand the vital nature of their roles. In past generations, caring for infants and toddlers may have been categorized as "babysitting." There were no formal degrees required for this position, and even young teenagers were perfectly capable of making sure that an infant stayed safe while the parent had to go to work.

Although keeping young children safe and healthy is still a primary goal for any caregiver, today's birth-to-toddler-aged classrooms should expect far more than safety. Trained caregivers can offer the infant safety, conversation, exploration, independence, and social skills. A trained caregiver can also assess if the infant is developing typically and assist the child with new challenges or refer the baby to a specialist to see if the child needs supportive therapy. The infant and toddler classroom is the birthplace for language skills and problem-solving. A caregiver in this classroom needs to be proud of these accomplishments and advocate for the importance of infant and toddler care.

Caregivers in the infant-toddler classroom must place a strong emphasis on relationships. Children need to feel safe and nurtured by their caregivers. Families need to trust the caregiver with whom they are leaving their children. Children need to know that when they cry or ask for support, the caregiver will respond. Caregivers need to talk to the children throughout the day, even when the children are not yet able to speak words. The creation of relationships will lead to many more developmental gains.

Caregivers in the infant and toddler classroom must be committed to professionalism. One of the key indicators of a quality infant or toddler classroom is consistent staffing. Young children need to see the same faces and have the same caregivers as frequently as possible. To create this consistency, caregivers must be committed to being in the classroom each day without frequent absences. It is also essential that all infant and toddler caregivers be committed to giving their time and attention in the classroom to the children, instead of talking to other adults or texting on a cell phone. To show how important this job truly is, it is essential for caregivers to devote all their time and energy to child successes.

Just like preschool and kindergarten teachers, infant and toddler caregivers need to be knowledgeable about child development milestones. This assists the caregiver with designing an appropriate classroom, providing toys that appeal to infants and toddlers, and planning activities to help each child overcome his or her next challenge. Child development knowledge also assists the caregiver to determine if a child is developing appropriately. If a child is consistently slow at meeting developmental milestones or significantly behind in one area of development, a knowledge of child development will help the caregiver assist the child or offer the family a referral for further evaluation of development.

FAMILY INVOLVEMENT IN THE INFANT AND TODDLER CLASSROOMS

Since the infant and toddler classrooms do not look like typical classrooms with desks and a teacher standing at the front of the classroom, families may not know how to participate in their young children's education. Of course, the parent must bring the child to the classroom each day and provide the caregiver with essential details about when the child last slept and about the child's last meal. Many families may not know how to participate in their infants' education beyond this point; however, family–caregiver partnerships are essential for the best possible care for children.

Families need to begin by finding out the best ways to communicate with the caregivers. They should find out how to call and check on their children during the day, and they should identify how the caregiver provides them with additional information about their growing children (e.g., email, classroom blog, weekly newsletter). It is also very valuable for families to take advantage of conferences with the caregivers, even in the infant classroom. Many adults may view conferences as a time when the teacher tells the family what the child has been doing wrong. That is not what a conference should be like in a quality childcare setting. A conference with the caregiver should be an opportunity for the family and the caregiver to share information about the child (i.e., what she likes, what calms her down, her preferences for sleep). This information-sharing process will allow the family and the caregiver to get to know the child as best as possible and prepare the most appropriate learning environment for her.

Families should also have opportunities to visit the classroom and watch their children play. Nursing mothers should have the option of coming and breastfeeding at intervals throughout the day. Families could also participate with the school environment as a whole by sitting on the advisory board or attending parent education nights.

LEARNING ABOUT INFANT AND TODDLER CARE

Quality care for infants and toddlers should involve the families and the caregivers. They should be working together to help the children learn in a loving environment. A quality classroom should not look like a smaller preschool classroom. Instead, the classroom should be designed to meet the needs of the young children in a flexible learning environment. In order to best prepare our kindergarten students to be ready for elementary school, caregivers must start working with our youngest children to help them learn essential skills that they will continue to develop throughout their educational career. This book will address each area of the infant and toddler classrooms and how that area further prepares a child to be ready for school success later in life.

Chapter One

Social and Emotional Skills

Social and emotional skills are the foundation of the early childhood classroom. The ability to play in groups with other children and learn the social rules of the classroom is an essential skill to prepare children for kindergarten. Many kindergarten teachers will tell parents that they are prepared to teach children their numbers and letters if they come to kindergarten without these skills. The teachers are trained to teach reading and counting, so that is part of their job description. However, it is *very* challenging for a kindergarten teacher when a child comes to school and is unable to follow simple directions or cooperate with other students in the classroom. Then the teacher must stop teaching academic skills to help the children with simpler social skills. Kindergarten teachers rely on early childhood educators to help children explore their emotions and learn to develop relationships before starting elementary school.

School readiness skills in the social and emotional domain include developing confidence, establishing relationships with teachers and peers, learning to communicate with teachers and other students, focusing on a task, persisting even when challenged, learning to express emotions, listening to instructions, following instructions, and paying attention (Parlakian, 2003). These skills begin in the infant classroom when children learn to establish attached relationships with caregivers and to interact with other children in the classroom. Toddlers then increase their social skills by attempting to share with other children and listen to their caregivers' directions.

THE IMPORTANCE OF RELATIONSHIPS

The National Association for the Education of Young Children has established ten traits that define a quality early childhood environment (NAEYC, 2008). One of these key traits is the program's ability to establish essential relationships. This can include relationships between the children and their caregivers, as well as the children and their peers. In the infant room, the key relationship is between the child and the adult that cares for that child. The secure, attached relationship between the caregiver and the children is the foundation of quality care in infant and toddler classrooms (Ebbeck and Yim, 2009). The nurturing and warm atmosphere provided by the caregiver can influence the child's ability to connect with the adult (Cryer, 2003).

Children are more likely to establish strong, attached relationships with caregivers they see each day. Having a consistent caregiver in the classroom each day can promote healthy social and emotional development, particularly with infants and younger toddlers (Holochwost et al., 2009). When children see the same caregivers again and again, they become familiar with those adults and begin to feel safe. Once the children feel safe and comfortable, then more complex characteristics of the relationships can begin to develop. Attachment is a key component to the language development process also. In a survey of childcare providers, all childcare staff that participated stated that being emotionally responsive to the child was one of the most important obligations of their jobs (Ebbeck and Yim, 2009).

Childcare centers achieve this type of emotional connection in different ways. The primary caregiver model, involving face-to-face interaction and holding the child throughout the day, seems to be the most popular method of establishing attachment with a small group of children (Ebbeck and Yim, 2009). When a caregiver works with a small group of young children each day, then she has the ability to learn when each child is hungry, how best to calm each child down to go to sleep, and what developmental goal is next for each child in the group. Babies flourish in her care accompanied by gentle touches, face-to-face interactions, and back-and-forth play between the child and the adult.

Infants are created to share in social interactions. This is often called "reciprocity." They are ready to seek out social engagement (Lewin-Benham, 2010). In fact, they thrive on it. Infants offer social interactions, and adults respond. Adults offer social interactions, and infants respond. Many of the interactions of young infants are nonverbal. Reciprocity involves cooing, conversation, tone of voice, movement, and facial expressions. Babies who are cared for by responsive adults develop secure attachments. These adults are attuned to the needs of each child.

TRUST

Erik Erikson, a notable developmental theorist, believed that the first year of life is the time period that children need to acquire basic trust. This means that infants feel safe and secure, with their caregivers and the world around them (Erikson, 1950). During this stage of life, when an infant cries, he needs to know that his caregiver will respond to his distress. When a child must rely on a caregiver for most of his needs, he must know that the caregiver will respond to his cries. This is the starting point of the attachment relationship. The adult must observe the child and learn his behavior in order to comfort him. Both the adult and the child must be invested so that adult–child interaction can create emotionally satisfying outcomes (Erikson, 1950).

Adult and child temperaments can be very different. It is essential for the adult to understand the differences in her own temperament and the temperament of the child. Basic trust comes from strong relationships. It requires responsive, predictable, and nurturing care from consistent caregivers to whom children show attachment (Greenman, Stonehouse, and Schweikert, 2008). Without this trust, the world is a very scary place to young children. All self-esteem and courage starts with this sense of basic trust. Many caregivers have opinions about holding a baby too much or what leads to "spoiling" a baby.

A *toddler* may learn to manipulate a caregiver by crying on demand in order to get the adult to react; however, an infant's cry is very different. An infant must learn to trust her caregiver, so the caregiver needs to be responsive when the infant is in distress. The newborn's desire to survive is the driving force that motivates the baby. The baby begins to trust when the caregiver responds to her. Trust is created when the baby feels safe, nurtured, supported, and secure in her survival. Trust is the foundation for all relationships (Butterfield, Martin, and Prairie, 2003).

An infant achieves a major developmental milestone when he enters into a close bond and nurturing relationship with both a parent and a trusted caregiver in the first year of life (Parlakian, 2003). These foundational relationships will be a safe place to which the child may return when he is scared of the environment or when he looks for reassurance after trying something new. When a supportive caregiver nurtures a young child, the child is able to trust, empathize, show compassion, demonstrate generosity, and establish a strong sense of right and wrong. Children develop self-direction, curiosity, persistence, cooperation, caring, and conflict resolution when adults have modeled healthy relationships.

Although several different caregivers may interact with the infant during the course of the day, typically there are some relationships that develop much deeper attachment. At home, the infant will form close relationships with her family members. In the classroom environment, there is usually one caregiver with whom the infant develops the strongest bond. The child's primary caregiver will be the classroom expert on the infant's emotional signals and will be able to calm the baby more easily than any other caregiver. She will be the caregiver that makes the baby feel safe and secure even when he is tired, hungry, or distressed. This caregiver will be an anchor for the child's emotional development while the infant is away from home (Butterfield, Martin, and Prairie, 2003).

RESPONSIVE CAREGIVING

Responsive care means that the caregiver creates a classroom environment that is safe and has established routines so that children learn what to expect. The caregiver provides a variety of materials for children to explore using their senses. The caregiver also engages in face-to-face interactions with the children and finds nurturing ways to meet their individual needs. The caregiver repeats these gentle and protective interactions each day to make the relationship stable and consistent. Young children then develop trust when they know they are a part of a secure relationship. The responsive caregiving that children receive during their early years has a direct impact on healthy brain development. When children experience positive interactions with responsive caregivers, they analyze emotional and behavioral responses, develop secure attachments, and learn how to resolve conflicts.

Responsive caregiving does not mean that the caregiver anticipates the child's every need and prevents the infant from ever experiencing distress. The infant does not learn trust if the caregiver meets every need before the child offers the signal. If that were to occur, the child would not learn trust, because the baby would never realize that he had a need to address. A child does not learn how to express his needs without momentary discomfort and the safety net of a reciprocal interaction (Butterfield, Martin, and Prairie, 2003).

To create a responsive caregiving environment, the caregiver can

- spend face-to-face time with babies, either with the baby sitting in the caregiver's lap or both sitting on the floor looking at one another
- spend time with toddlers modeling dramatic play activities and observing their social interactions
- observe a child before he or she engages with him. The caregiver needs to learn how that individual child interacts with his environment and the other children in the classroom. What are his emotional signals when he is upset?

- respect the children in the classroom. The caregiver should allow them to play and interact with what interests them. He should be a resource when the children need him, but he should always allow them to try something independently first.
- try to figure out what type of message the child is sending. The caregiver should look at all the different methods of communication: facial expressions, gestures, coos, simple words, and movements.
- make sure to observe the child's behavior at different times during the day. The caregiver should make sure to look for behaviors that center around feedings, diapering, and sleep routines. It is important to look for physical and vocal cues that children repeat during these daily routines.

This type of interaction and observation will help the caregiver understand the child with a deeper perspective. Then he can respond to the child's needs in the most appropriate manner. The details about the child's wants, needs, preferences, and interests are the facts that allow caregivers to individualize their response to each child in the classroom.

DEVELOPING SOCIAL SKILLS

In order to guide infants and toddlers through their social development, it is essential that all infant and toddler caregivers understand the developmental milestones for social skills.

- *Birth to two months:* A newborn infant can identify the scent of her mother and father and her primary caregiver, as well as the sound of their voices. The infant will act differently when she is being held by one of her foundational caregivers compared with a new adult. The infant's social development begins when the child can recognize the differences between others. An infant begins to self-regulate in the first two months. She can learn to tune out large amounts of stimulation when she is overwhelmed, and she may pay attention to one specific person or object when something seems new and interesting.
- *Two to four months:* A nonmobile infant may begin to explore during this time. He can begin reaching out for familiar adults, engage with a caregiver, and show interest in his own face in a mirror. He begins discovering that his actions can affect others.
- *Four to six months:* Infants can consistently differentiate between an essential caregiver and a stranger. The infant begins to cooperate more during daily tasks like dressing, eating, or diapering. Also, an infant may begin

to copy facial expressions and actions, such as smiling at a smiling adult, sticking out her tongue, or playing peek-a-boo.
- *Six to nine months:* Stranger anxiety develops at this age, and the infant attempts to obtain the primary caregiver's attention constantly. Infants can secure themselves to a familiar adult and hide their faces when introduced to strangers. Stranger anxiety is an appropriate developmental milestone. Infants understand that they feel secure with their primary caregivers, so they quickly return to them when presented with an unfamiliar person or situation.
- *Nine to twelve months:* Infants begin to identify the connection between the caregiver and having their individual needs met. This means the infant may turn to the caregiver and begin to fuss when she needs something. This is her attempt to directly communicate with her caregiver in the hope that the caregiver will respond. Infants will also begin to use one-word utterances. Initially these one-word phrases may only be understood by the essential caregivers. Others will be able to understand the baby's communication with time.
- *Thirteen to twenty-three months:* Toddlers want to explore the environment, but they still see the world as their own. They want to explore the classroom and take in information, but they are only starting to realize that others are sharing their space. Young toddlers will gain language skills and begin to interact with others, but they are still only interested in the world as it affects their wants and needs. Toddlers are protective of their toys and their caregivers. Everything important belongs solely to them and no one else.

  As the year progresses, they will begin to identify when a classmate is upset, but they will not yet know how to react to those emotions. Toddlers also begin to imitate the actions of those around them. They strive for independence and may refuse help from adults (even when it is necessary). When a toddler is not allowed to do exactly what he wants, he may throw a tantrum since he is not completely in control of his emotions or his body.
- *Twenty-four to thirty-six months:* There is a great deal of growth that occurs between the ages of two and three years. Older toddlers begin to show affection, and they can identify basic emotions in the faces of others. Although she can still not show empathy for others, an older toddler may be able to share one of her toys for a short amount of time. She may also have several friends that she prefers to interact with at school. This is a period of rapid language acquisition, so a child may be learning new words each day. Increased language skills will improve socialization skills and improve the toddler's ability to cooperate and play together.

ENCOURAGING SOCIAL SKILLS

As children begin developing social skills, it is a key task of the caregiver to encourage this process. The caregiver must consider how the environment is set up to encourage social interaction, and the adults in the room must be a part of the social interaction to model the behavior that they want to see the children demonstrate. With infants, it is essential that the caregiver give each baby as much face-to-face time as possible during those first few months. That may mean that the caregiver is sitting on the floor holding one baby in her arms beside another infant in a bouncy seat. The caregiver can engage in conversation with both babies and take turns making eye contact with each of them. When infants get this face-to-face time, they will study the caregiver's face and attempt to copy the facial expressions they see.

It is also important for the infant to start spending time with less familiar adults. It is typical for infants to show separation anxiety when they are separated from a preferred caregiver, but it is also healthy to become comfortable with new adults. When a new caregiver comes into the classroom to assist with breaks or offer additional classroom support, it is a good time to let the new caregiver hold the infant for a short period of time and begin to desensitize the child from this stranger anxiety. If the infant remains upset, then he can still return to the arms of the familiar adult to calm down. This process should improve as the primary caregiver leaves the room for short intervals and the infant learns to remain calm.

Toddlers are learning to be around other children in the classroom, but they still are not capable of sharing and taking turns. To help young toddlers enjoy being in a classroom with other children, it is important to have duplicate toys so that more than one child can play with the same material. Caregivers will still need to intervene between toddlers when they become frustrated, but this is one way to reduce these frustrations.

Toddlers also need to learn the social cues of others in order to interact with multiple children in the same classroom. You can begin this process by looking at the faces in picture books and asking the children what they think these people are feeling. Ask toddlers if they can make a mad face, a happy face, and a scared face. Mirror play is a great way to begin identifying facial expression. The caregiver can also provide baby dolls with different facial expressions for children to hold and comfort.

Caregivers can help children identify the emotions in someone's tone of voice by demonstrating what vocal expressions someone may use when going through these emotions. If a caregiver wants to demonstrate a happy voice, he can use high, melodic tones. If the caregiver is demonstrating that he is sad, he can use a low, soft, dejected voice. To show the toddlers what angry sounds like, the caregiver can use a loud, tense, and strained voice.

PLAYING WITH OTHERS

As toddlers mature, they will be more interested in interacting with the other children in their classroom. The caregiver needs to model appropriate social behavior and be a part of these social interactions. Also, when the caregiver is close to the children, she can easily intervene when toddlers begin to disagree.

Young infants and toddlers begin the process of playing with others when they start observing the other children in their environment. Initially they will not interact with the other children, but they will begin to study their actions to watch what other children are doing and learn their movements so they can eventually imitate the actions of those around them.

When children progress to parallel play, infants and toddlers will sit close to one another but still keep to themselves. Parallel play is an individual activity. One child will occasionally watch a classmate as he chews on a foam block to see what he is doing or even to admire his toy, but most of her time is spent concentrating on her own toys and her own actions. This does not mean she doesn't enjoy being around the other children. She is now familiar enough with her peers that she enjoys being close to them, even if she isn't ready to play with them yet.

When toddlers move to the stage of associative play, they begin to play with the same materials in the same area and even share toys, even though they may not be playing together. A table full of toddlers may all be sitting down to play with playdough. The toddlers can share cookie cutters to create playdough shapes, but they are not cooperatively creating shapes and characters for the same story. They are still playing individually. Likewise, several toddlers may all be playing in the kitchen area of the classroom. One toddler may be playing with a baby doll, and another may be pretending to cook in the kitchen. Even though the toddlers are in the kitchen together, they are not a part of the same story.

As young toddlers mature and eventually begin to play together in the same areas of the classroom, this can lead to arguments since they are still learning to share and negotiate with one another. It is the caregiver's job to assist children with learning how to share, take turns, and be friends with one another. Here are some strategies that will assist children through this stage of social development:

- *Set the example:* **Caregivers need to participate in play with the children. When the caregiver is in the block center or dressing up in the pretend play**

center, she needs to set the example of how to share. The caregiver needs to ask before picking up a toy that a child has been using. The caregiver also needs to say thank you when a toddler gives her a turn. Caregivers need to praise toddlers every time they are willing to share or wait for a classmate to take a turn first. The caregiver also needs to practice using please and thank you so that children can see those concrete examples of adults using their manners.
- *Choose cooperative activities:* Caregivers need to find activities that allow children to be a team. Toddlers need to participate in group art projects where they all make thumbprints or paint with strings on the same large piece of paper. Older toddlers can participate in a classroom cooking project or make music together as a classroom band. These group activities will encourage teamwork and sharing.
- *Be prepared to intervene:* Caregivers need to be sitting on the floor in close proximity to children so they can step in at a moment's notice. Although toddlers are interested in playing with other children, they still lack the language skills and self-control to negotiate properly when a situation doesn't go their way. This can lead to impulsive reactions like hitting or biting a peer. Caregivers need to keep a close eye on all the toddlers during playtime and be ready to step in quickly if anyone prepares to lash out at a friend. Caregivers can then redirect the frustrated toddlers to a new activity or guide them through a negotiation.
- *Practice, practice, practice:* It can take months and months before toddlers can navigate a playtime that does not end in tears and tantrums. Learning social skills takes time and patience. Caregivers need to continue to provide social opportunities for young children so they can learn strategies to get along with their peers.
- *Don't forget to make each child feel special:* Even if your focus is on helping children play together, remember to still give individual attention to each child and acknowledge their accomplishments. Give infants and toddlers both plenty of physical affection by holding them, rocking them, sitting them in your lap to read books, and offering them hugs. Children who feel safe and secure in their environment are more likely to interact with new people. Classroom routines like helping a child drift off to sleep or changing diapers is a great place to talk to him one-on-one or give him special attention.
- *Read stories about friends and families:* Reading a book with a small group of children is a time to promote being together and talking about relationships. When reading a book to infants and toddlers, the caregiver needs to choose a book with large pictures and a limited amount of words to keep the children engaged. These books should show families or friends playing together and enjoying themselves. The caregiver needs to point out

the facial expressions of the people in the book and what they are doing together. He should ask toddlers if the characters are happy and what they are playing. He should also reinforce that families care about each other and enjoy being together.
- *Encourage taking turns:* Caregivers need to set up the classroom environment to allow toddlers to take turns. Toddlers do not need to wait for long periods of time because they could become too frustrated. They can learn to wait for a friend to do something first. For example, it is appropriate for two toddlers to take turns going down the playground slide. Toddlers can take turns on the swing when one child gets to swing and the other gets to push. Toddlers in the pretend play area can take turns wearing the princess dress.

Toddlers who get experience sharing with their friends will mature to preschoolers who can play cooperatively and begin to show empathy for their classmates. Toddlers who understand the rules of taking turns will grow into preschoolers who understand how to listen and follow the classroom teacher's instructions. With a strong foundation of social skills, children are much more likely to be successful when they begin their elementary school education.

Chapter Two

The Importance of Routines

Early childhood caregivers frequently talk about the importance of routines. They encourage families to establish routines at home in order to create consistency and help young children feel safe. Infant and toddler classrooms establish routines to help children transition from home to school and move through the day with trust and confidence. Despite encouragement to establish routines, caregivers and families can easily be confused about whether or not a routine is a timed classroom schedule or an event that occurs throughout the day.

WHAT ARE ROUTINES?

Routines can be defined as repeated, predictable events that are established as part of a child's daily tasks (Gillespie and Petersen, 2012). These routines can be individualized to meet the needs of each child in the classroom. For example, one child's naptime routine may involve getting his stuffed bunny out of his backpack, lying down on his cot, and letting the caregiver cover him up with a blanket and then pat his back until he falls asleep. His routine may be slightly different from that of the other children in the classroom, even though all of the toddlers in the room are preparing for a nap. A child's routine should match his level of independence, his ability to self-regulate, and his basic needs (e.g., how tired he is on a particular day). The sequence of the routine will stay the same from day to day, but the timing and the caregiver's accommodations may change based on the child's needs.

The classroom schedule for infants and toddlers includes arrival, breakfast, free play and exploration, lunchtime, napping, snack, and departure. Diapering will be included throughout the schedule based on the needs of the children. Also, outdoor playtime will be included in the schedule based on the age of the children and the program's playground schedule. Younger infant rooms will frequently have two naptimes, and older toddler rooms will typically have two outdoor playtimes. The classroom schedule is the outer framework for the day, but individual children will need that schedule to be flexible in order to meet their needs (Gillespie and Petersen, 2012). Each family arrives at a different time. Infants have individualized eating and sleeping needs. Still, when the caregivers begin to put each baby to sleep, they use a predictable routine that meets the needs of the infant.

These predictable routines are meaningful to young children. They help put children at ease and allow them to self-soothe, all while meeting their basic needs. Research shows that daily routines create predictable and less stressful environments for infants and toddlers and improve behavior during classroom hours (American Academy of Sleep Medicine, 2009). The most common classroom routines for young children include separating from the family, eating, playing, and sleeping.

- *Separating from the family:* When children arrive at the classroom each day, they need to be greeted by a consistent caregiver. They will separate more easily from a family member when they trust the caregiver waiting for them. Once the parent has passed the child to the caregiver, it is important to establish a transition routine. For a toddler, this could be going to the window to wave goodbye to Mom as she drives away. For an infant, this routine could include sitting down to rock or being held until the child is ready to get down on the floor and explore the classroom.
- *Eating:* Infants and toddlers spend a lot of time eating. A young infant may eat as frequently as every two hours. Some infants struggle with feeding issues like acid reflux, and some toddlers may already be developing the habits of a picky eater. Infants will be most at ease when they learn that when they are hungry, their caregiver feeds them. It is important that meals with infants and toddlers include a pleasant atmosphere. A caregiver needs to find a comforting place to feed an infant, like in a rocking chair in a dimly lit corner of the room to allow the baby to focus on eating. Toddlers need an encouraging mealtime filled with conversation and the caregiver modeling the appropriate mealtime behavior.
- *Playing:* Every child needs playtime each day to explore the classroom. Young children learn by using their senses to take in information, so they need to be offered a play environment that allows them to put toys in their mouth, hear pleasant sounds, and see a variety of shapes and colors. Even though infants may be in the same classroom every day, exploring is still an adventure. In order to make the infant or young toddler feel safe, the caregiver needs to be a secure base that the child returns to if she becomes

scared or frustrated. This means that the playtime routine includes the caregiver sitting on the floor and participating in playtime.

This also means that the caregiver will model how to use the toys or assist a child with the classroom materials in order to help her move to the next stages of understanding. Every child moves and explores differently, so the caregiver must allow the child time each day to become comfortable with the new environment. This may mean that the child initially sits in the caregiver's lap before deciding to crawl around the room on her own.
- *Sleeping:* One of the most important routines of the day is helping an infant or toddler go to sleep. In order to establish consistency, it is helpful to put the child to sleep around the same time each day. Once a baby is overtired, it is harder to calm him down. At the same time, if a small child needs to sleep earlier in the day than usual, the caregiver needs to follow his lead.

In order to help follow an established sleep routine, the caregiver needs to watch for signs that the child is sleepy (e.g., drowsy eyelids, yawning, rubbing eyes, or becoming cranky). Once the caregiver can see that the infant or toddler needs to go to sleep, she should begin to follow the child's normal routine. For an infant, this may include having a bottle and rocking in a chair before falling asleep. For a toddler, a sleep routine may include giving the child more independence like having her take off her shoes, get her blanket, and lay down on her cot before the caregiver begins to rub her back.

BENEFITS FOR CHILDREN

Infants and toddlers grow at a rapid pace during the first three years of life. They are rushing through many different physical milestones like sitting, crawling, walking, and running. At the same time, the brain is growing faster than it will at any other stage of development (Berk, 2012). Infants and toddlers are learning to explore their environment and to interact with their caregivers. All of this work requires the child to get large amounts of rest, adequate sleep, and comfort from a supportive caregiver.

A child's current stage of development (or the child's natural temperament) can make it challenging for him to get the amount of rest, food, or relaxation required to meet his basic needs (Snyder, 2016). As the baby goes through a growth spurt, he may need more food and rest than usual. His natural temperament may make it more challenging for a caregiver to soothe him to sleep. However, a familiar routine may alleviate additional stress for the child.

When children are in a classroom environment with familiar voices and recognize the same comforting smell of the caregiver that soothes them each day, they are more capable of expressing their needs and calming themselves down once their needs are met. Babies will typically cry when they are hungry, tired, or uncomfortable. If a familiar caregiver learns the infant's cues, then they are less likely to get extremely upset. The caregiver will respond to the child's needs as soon as she notices the familiar cues. When the same caregivers care for the child each day, they will use the same routine to feed the child or rock her to sleep. Once this familiar routine begins (e.g., the caregiver picks the infant up, goes to the rocking chair, lays the baby down in her arms) the infant will begin to self-soothe before the need is completely met. The baby knows what to expect and calms down because she trusts the caregiver.

Babies need to know that they can trust their caregivers. When caregivers use the same routines every day, the children learn to trust through repeated positive experiences. Not only do routines help infants and toddlers overcome the stress of hunger and fatigue, but the positive benefits of routine also continue to solidify the strong bond between the child and the caregiver. Reinforcing this trusting relationship creates the foundation of many future relationships with caregivers and peers, all based on trust. When the routines at home mirror the routines in the classroom, then trust can be established even more quickly.

Routines can also help children improve their social skills with their peers and less familiar adults. When children learn the routines for greetings, they begin to wave and say hello to everyone they see. Likewise, when infants and toddlers learn the routine for departures, they begin to say goodbye or offer hugs to those in the room. These routines teach young children how they need to interact, and this typically helps them further develop their social skills.

Routines also have the ability to help children develop their self-control and reduce potential power struggles between the child and the caregiver. If a consistent classroom routine is established, then the child begins to understand what to expect. If a toddler anticipates a sequence of events (e.g., lunchtime, diaper change, and naptime), then they are less likely to resist any particular event. He is not scared of what might possibly be happening next and feels comfortable with the established plan. This structured plan frequently reduces the need for a child to argue with an adult about whether or not it is naptime.

BENEFITS FOR FAMILIES

Established routines in the classroom benefit the families as well as the children. Many toddlers will demonstrate separation anxiety when their family members drop them off in the classroom; however, an established arrival routine will make these separations easier on the child. This, in turn, will reduce the stress level of the family member.

Because of the nature of family life, a child's home schedule may be less predictable than the classroom schedule. However, if the routines in the classroom mirror the routines in the home, then the family can still reduce the amount of stress that a child experiences during major transitions that occur throughout the day (e.g., leaving the house, mealtime, bedtime). Again, when the child experiences less stress, the stress levels of the family members also go down.

Research suggests that when children have established routines, the parents typically feel more competent with their ability to care for the child (American Academy of Sleep Medicine, 2009). This is easy to understand since routines eliminate additional stress, help meet the child's basic needs, and help the child learn to self-soothe. Again, routines also strengthen the bond between the adult and the child, and therefore the family members experience confidence when the children show that they trust their family to take care of them. Since the family can benefit greatly from established routines, caregivers need to encourage them to put routines in place and guide them through creating those routines.

The same research also shows that maternal stress levels decrease when routines are established. The beginning of parenthood can be very stressful. It requires the parents to redesign their lifestyles completely. Establishing routines benefits the parents because they also need to embrace the familiar. Parents may find comfort when they feed their infants each day in the same cozy chair. They may look forward to a family dinner each night after a long day of work. These routines establish a new sense of trust for adults after their lives have been completely altered to meet the needs of their children.

ESTABLISHING A CLASSROOM ROUTINE

Routines are individualized to the classroom and to each student in the classroom, but there are several tips that can help caregivers create predictable, repeatable routines in their infant and toddler classrooms:

- *Encourage family members to create their own routines for arrival and pick-up times.* This will allow the family to be involved with comforting the child through these transitions, and it will make the transition easier on the family and the child.
- *Keep routines predictable and consistent.* Children respond best to routines when caregivers do the same predictable sequence of events over and over. Then the child is not worried about what is going to happen next. If the

caregiver sings the same song every day when it is time to pick up the toys, then the child understands what to do and knows what is coming next.
- *Create routines based on the age of the children.* Children possess different skills at different ages, so the caregiver needs to understand what they need at each developmental level. Infants may be on their own schedule, but a group of toddlers may be able to share the same routine for the entire classroom. Once the children have moved into the toddler room, they can probably share the same schedule for eating and sleeping; however, the caregivers may still need to individualize some routines to help each child fall asleep.
- *Children need routines in a group and routines that allow them to be alone.* The classroom environment needs to be set up in a way that will offer children individual learning experiences and opportunities to be around others. Even though infants and young toddlers may not be interacting with other children in the classroom, they still need the opportunity to observe others while they play.
- *Children need routines with rest time and active playtime.* Infants and toddlers are both learning motor skills whether they are practicing rolling over or learning to jump and climb. They need opportunities throughout the day to practice these skills. At the same time, all young children need opportunities to rest. This can be in the form of a group naptime for a toddler, or an infant may need to rest in a caregiver's arms after spending ten minutes lying on the floor on her belly lifting her head up.
- *Create routines for challenging parts of the day.* There are always parts of the daily schedule that are more challenging than others. For example, the transition for a toddler classroom to put on their coats and go outside may be complicated because the children all want to go outside and it is hard to wait for the caregivers to help each child put on a coat. This is a great time of day for a planned routine. Caregivers can use a special song or a pleasant sound like a chime to let the children know it is time to get their coats and line up at the door to the playground. This can alleviate a lot of unnecessary confusion when the children know what to do as soon as they are given a predictable cue.

FLEXIBLE SCHEDULES FOR INFANTS AND TODDLERS

Although it is important to have predictable routines with infants and toddlers, it is also important to remember to keep the classroom schedule flexible enough to meet the needs of the children. For example, as infants grow into young toddlers, their eating and sleeping schedule will begin to change. A baby may need only one long nap in the middle of the day instead of two short naps. An infant will begin eating more table food and rely less on bottles or breastfeeding. During these transitions, it is very important to follow the child's cues. Once the caregiver has spent ten to fifteen minutes attempting to put the child to sleep for a morning nap, it may be time to move on to the next item on the daily schedule.

Many young children will often have a hard time readjusting to the classroom after a vacation or illness. Once the child has had a break from his typical routine, it may take several days to reestablish that pattern. Different temperaments handle these changes in different ways, but most children will take only a few days to feel comfortable in the classroom again.

It is also important to remember that many children will have a difficult time responding to their predictable routines and daily schedules if their basic needs are not being met. If a child comes to school and did not sleep the night before, the top priority is to give her the opportunity to sleep, even if it is not her normal rest time. If a child comes to school and is desperately hungry, then it becomes the top priority to feed him, even if it is not mealtime. Even though caregivers may not know about the home lives of the children they care for, if it appears that one of the children is not getting his or her basic needs met due to any reason (e.g., a family emergency, lack of housing, limited resources), it is essential to address those needs regardless of the typical schedule.

SLEEP ROUTINES

Sleep routines are probably the most important routines in infant and toddler classrooms. Caregivers want to establish a caring and nurturing routine to help put a child to sleep, but it is also important to make sure that the child, especially an infant, remains safe. One of the leading causes of infant death is sudden infant death syndrome. Although these deaths cannot be attributed to any one cause, many of them have been linked to unsafe sleeping arrangements. All caregivers must be aware of the "safe sleep" requirements established by the American Academy of Pediatrics.

- Infants need to be placed to sleep on their backs for every sleep situation (Moon, 2016).
- Infants need to sleep on a firm sleep surface like a mattress, not large pillows or stuffed animals.
- There should be no loose bedding or stuffed animals in the crib with the infant. The safest setting is to only have a fitted sheet in the crib with the baby.

- Infants may have a pacifier in the crib while sleeping, but it must be put in the infant's mouth while the infant is still awake. Also, there should be no pacifier clip or string in the crib with the infant.
- Caregivers need to periodically check on the infant while she is sleeping. Make sure that the infant is not overheating while asleep.
- Caregivers need to supervise any playtime closely when a young infant is lying on his tummy. Once the baby begins to tire, it is easy to rest his face on the floor and cover the nose and mouth. In this situation, it is safest to place him in a resting position.

When a caregiver is trying to create healthy sleeping routines in the classroom, it is important to know what to expect from young babies. Infants typically have about one hour of alert time followed by two to three hours of sleeping (Karp, 2002). During alert time, the infant may be eating, crying, or observing the environment. The longest periods of sleep will probably be at night and last up to four hours.

Although toddlers may thrive on a schedule, infants are much different. The whole concept of scheduling an infant's sleep is a very new one in the course of history (Karp, 2002). A child has the ability to adapt to a sleep routine early in life if he is mature enough to achieve delayed gratification. Some infants want to be fed immediately or held immediately, so it is more challenging to place those infants on a strict schedule. As the infant matures, it is more likely that he will acquire a regular pattern to eating and sleeping. A child over the age of one will more likely follow a structured sleep schedule; however, some children may still struggle with regular sleep patterns due to medical issues like chronic ear infections or acid reflux.

Chapter Three

Infant and Toddler Language Skills

Language is a skill that a child starts acquiring before being born. As a baby grows and develops in utero, he or she begins to learn the distinct differences between the mother's voice and other voices in the background. Once the baby is born, the sound of the mother's voice is one of the first sounds that help the baby attach to the mother. Young infants use different cries to attract adult attention and repeat sounds that they hear frequently and those that are reinforced by adults. Since these early language skills begin to develop at such a young age, it is essential for infant and toddler classrooms to start cultivating language skills as soon as a new baby is enrolled in an early childhood program.

Language acquisition is a complicated process, but it is essential to many areas of development. One aspect of language acquisition is children learning to duplicate the varied sounds heard throughout their environment. Initially, this may sound like cooing. A child repeats the consonant sounds and then the vowel sounds that he or she hears, without any connection to the meaning of the sound. As children mature, they may repeat phrases or expressions they hear in conversation. Sometimes they know the meaning of the words or expressions, and other times they may choose to repeat them simply because they enjoy the sound.

At a young age a child also learns about voice tone and gestures as a way to communicate. When a child is as young as six months of age, he may be able to respond to the change of tone in someone else's voice. He can also begin to alter his own voice to show pleasure or displeasure. Eighteen-month-old children can use simple hand gestures to express themselves, even if they are not able to use a wide variety of words.

Vocabulary development begins in infancy. Children listen to the vocabulary used in their environment. Around the age of one, a child is capable of saying her first words. The amount of vocabulary a child uses at a young age is directly linked to the amount of vocabulary that she hears (Hart and Risley, 1995). These words may begin as one-syllable utterances, but they develop into full words and complete thoughts as she hears the people around her continue to have conversations, read books, and sing songs.

Infants and toddlers also learn about conversation skills at a very young age. They begin to understand concepts like turn-taking in a conversation in their infancy. They hear adults speak to them, and they coo in response. They may answer a question with an excited squeal or by gesturing to indicate the toys or food that they want. As their vocabulary increases, children begin to answer questions with yes or no responses, and eventually they use a full statement. Young children constantly observe adults having conversations with one another. They learn skills like turn-taking, but they also learn how close to stand to someone during a conversation, how loudly to speak, and how to offer a response that answers the question asked.

Young children use vocabulary and language skills in all areas of development. Vocabulary helps children identify objects around them. Conversation skills help them to be curious and ask questions about the world around them. Communication skills assist them with developing social relationships. It is essential that all young children are a part of a language-rich environment (an environment filled with verbal and printed words) so that they can advance their speech and preliteracy skills. The quality of childcare that a child receives in an infant or toddler classroom can either enhance or hinder this language development (Vernon-Feagans et al., 2007).

THE HART AND RISLEY STUDY

In 1995, Drs. Betty Hart and Todd Risley from the University of Kansas published groundbreaking research linking early language experiences to what is now known as the "achievement gap." Hart and Risley studied the amount and types of language interactions to which children were exposed in their homes during their early childhood and how that affected their development. They found that children from affluent families heard almost three hundred more words per hour than children from families in the lowest socioeconomic bracket. Over the four years of the study, this created a thirty-million-word difference between children from the affluent families and children from the at-risk families (Hart and Risley, 1995).

Along with the number of words that children heard during the four years the study was conducted, the researchers noticed several crucial trends. First, the more words that families spoke to their children, the faster the children's vocabularies increased (Hart and Risley, 1995). Then as their vocabularies increased, their IQ scores also increased. Likewise, the less the parents spoke to the children, the less the children spoke in general.

Second, the families that spoke the most words to their children also showed other positive language traits. These homes exposed children to more diverse language by using more comparative language and synonyms for words the children already knew (Hart and Risley, 1995). Families also used more complex vocabulary in front of the children. This helped the children to advance their vocabulary.

Third, the higher socioeconomic families used more positive language with the children. Instead of constantly using vocabulary to discipline young children, these families used language to encourage their children and demonstrate the skills that the family wanted them to exhibit (Hart and Risley, 1995). Instead of using the word "No" over and over again, the affluent families gave the children a detailed description of what they were requesting from them. This allowed the children to hear additional vocabulary instead of a one-word response, and it also let the children view language as a teaching tool instead of as a punishment.

The researchers also noticed that more affluent families had frequent back-and-forth conversations with their children (Hart and Risley, 1995). This encouraged the children to ask questions and explore concepts for higher-level thinking. In lower-income homes, the families used short phrases or one-word responses to instruct their children, but there were fewer opportunities for conversations and questions.

Looking at the results of this research, many of these concepts apply to the infant and toddler classroom. In a quality infant classroom, children should be exposed to a large amount of vocabulary. They should have the opportunity to hear positive language and engage in conversations appropriate to their level of participation. Caregivers should use a wide variety of vocabulary words and describe the events that are occurring in the classroom in order to increase the children's language skills. These are the traits that will prepare young children for successful school experiences in the future.

INFANT AND TODDLER LANGUAGE RESEARCH

To further support the research from the 1995 Hart and Risley study, additional research was published in 2015 that continued to emphasize the achievement gap established by the time a child starts kindergarten. This longitudinal study looked at the oral language skills of young children from infancy through age five.

The research team conducted academic assessments of the children and interviewed the families of the children at nine, twenty-four, forty-eight, and sixty months. Again, the results showed that children raised in lower socioeconomic settings had much smaller vocabularies and were less prepared for kindergarten. This study also demonstrated that the oral language vocabulary that the children had at twenty-four months of age was indicative of their academic skills when entering kindergarten (Morgan et al., 2015). This means that waiting for a quality preschool experience may not be enough. The quality of the infant and toddler care a child receives can either contribute to or limit early language development. Quality early childhood education must begin during infancy, and a foundational component of this education program is a heavy emphasis on language skills.

RESPONSIVE LANGUAGE AND CONVERSATION SKILLS

Language has many different uses in the early childhood classroom. When children are very young, the caregiver may use language to label many of the items in the room so that the infant can begin to associate each item with a specific word. Long before a child can say the word, he or she may still know the name of the object. When the adult says the name of a person or toy, the baby will immediately turn her eyes and focus on the object that was named. This type of language learning is more like a quiz game to help the child memorize the sounds of a new word. This is a foundational element of learning language.

The next step in teaching language skills is when the caregiver chooses his or her language on the response of the child. Instead of simply assisting the child with word memorization, responsive language becomes the first step toward conversation skills. If a young infant coos, then the caregiver may respond by making eye contact with the child and playfully asking what the baby wants. If the baby screams, then the caregiver will attempt to use a calming voice and pick the child up to show the baby that he or she is there to assist.

Every time the caregiver responds to a young child, the baby has the potential to develop more synaptic connections as she discovers the cause-and-effect relationship of communication (Bardige, 2016). As the brain grows and the synapse connections increase, the child learns to decode language, interpret tone and nonverbal communication, problem-solve, and self-regulate.

When adults begin to have responsive language interactions with infants, they are typically using Parentese or infant-directed speech. When adults use Parentese, they are still using correct vocabulary, but the tone and inflection of the voice changes. The pitch of the adult voice is higher and may sound melodic. The vowel sounds are longer. The phrases are short, and they primarily include nouns and verbs instead of long passages of complicated vocabulary. Because of the melodic and high-pitched tones used for Parentese, infants are drawn into the conversation and make more eye contact with the adult.

If the adult is using responsive language correctly, then he can tell by the infant's coos, tone of voice, facial expression, and body language how to respond to the baby. After the adult speaks, he allows for a pause so that the infant has an opportunity to respond. For a very young child, this is typically a scream or a coo, but it is still the infant's opportunity to communicate. Creating an environment for turn-taking with the earliest conversations also allows children greater language skills once they begin to master using words.

By the time most babies are three months old, they have learned how to engage an adult in a back-and-forth interaction (Bardige, 2016). The more often the adult responds to the child's initiation, the stronger the foundation of trust that develops between the child and the adult. The babies that hear more words and learn how to participate in "conversations" between the ages of two and six months are the toddlers that possess a larger vocabulary at two years of age (Gilkerson and Richards, 2009).

Toddlers best learn new words by participating in active conversations (Tamis-LeMonda, Kuckirko, and Song, 2014). Contingent communication, with adults responding promptly and in an individualized way to children's comments, creates the skeleton of a conversation where children learn to think about what the other person said before creating their own response. When children have ample opportunities for conversation and child-directed thoughts, they develop more speed in conversations and larger vocabularies to participate in these conversations (Weisleder and Fernald, 2013).

The need for active conversations is one of the reasons why pediatricians caution parents against exposing infants and toddlers to screen time. Children will hear a variety of words on the television, but since the screen does not provide a contingent response to the child, the toddler may have no context for what the television is saying. Also, as pictures on the television are two-dimensional (flat) images, children do not see them the same as the real thing.

For example, the television may be showing a picture of a ball and offering the vocabulary, but since the picture does not look the same as a real ball, the child may still have difficulty associating the real ball with the label. Finally, when children are spending time in front of a screen, they are not participating in live conversation. That is common for adults as well. As soon as adults sit down to watch a television show, the conversation stops. If a child is spending time in front of a screen at a young age, then he or she is losing valuable conversation time that could help increase vocabulary.

Caregivers must provide responsive communication in order to encourage young children to participate in conversations, but it is also essential for childcare providers in the classroom to model conversations for young children. Caregivers should have frequent conversations throughout the day that model proper grammar and etiquette. A quality early childhood language environment will show caregivers demonstrating essential conversational skills such as

- taking turns in a conversation;
- answering when someone asks them a question;
- noticing nonverbal body cues, signals, and gestures and then responding;
- introducing a topic into a conversation so the listener can understand;
- staying on the subject of a conversation;
- maintaining the right amount of eye contact;
- having a conversation with another person without giving attention to an electronic device;
- using different communication styles that suit different communicative partners; and
- learning that in certain situations you should not talk.

These conversations are not skills that an infant will be able to duplicate; however, it is essential for a child to have a role model. Young children imitate information, so it is important for them to witness a role model before they learn to speak independently. Infants and toddlers also need to hear conversations in a variety of settings. For example, they need to hear conversations between two people and conversations in a large group. They need to witness conversations between two adults and conversations between an adult and a child. They also need to see playful conversations where the speaker can use a loud voice, and they need to see more respectful conversations that require a softer speaking voice. All of these models prepare a child for the conversations that he or she will have in the future.

Caregivers can also use conversations with toddlers as an opportunity to expand on the children's current language skills. If a toddler makes a short statement like "dog go," then the caregiver can respond by saying, "Yes, the dog is going to get the ball." When the caregiver agrees with the child's statement, she is reinforcing the child's language skills. When the caregiver adds additional content to the child's statement, she is offering the child an opportunity to hear additional vocabulary related to the situation. When a caregiver responds and expands on a toddler's statements, she is modeling more advanced forms of conversation and vocabulary to help the child increase language skills.

EXPOSURE TO ADVANCED LANGUAGE

When infants first begin to speak, their first words are typically people or items of the utmost importance. They use words to label the people in their lives or to draw attention to the items in their environment. As their vocabulary begins to grow, they are still using their words to label other items. Parents show the baby pictures of animals on the farm or in the zoo and repeat the same words over and over until the child associates the picture with the word. Infants often find that they can use the same word to get many different results (Gopnik, Meltzoff, and Kuhl, 1999). For example, when a young child says the word "Mommy," he may want Mommy to hold him, he may be identifying Mommy as she comes to pick him up from childcare, or he may simply want Mommy to give him her attention.

Parents and caregivers have been cautioned against using baby talk (made-up words with rhyming syllables) when talking to young children because the children will begin to imitate them and use the made-up words instead of proper grammar. This does not mean that caregivers can use only small words and phrases when talking with young children. Again, children often learn by imitation, so it is important to begin exposing young children to a large variety of vocabulary words starting from their infancy.

A research study in 2006 found that even though infants and young toddlers may not be speaking yet, they are still actively learning the language that they hear spoken in their environment. The research study specifically observed ten-month-old babies who had not yet spoken their first words. When the researchers used a voice tone that drew the baby's attention and paired the new vocabulary word with the item that the baby was looking at, they found that the baby learned the meanings of new words after hearing them only twice (Pruden et al., 2006).

If young infants and toddlers absorb new vocabulary after only two contextual repetitions, then caregivers have the opportunity to increase their language acquisition at a very young age. Infant and toddler caregivers can increase vocabulary by simply substituting synonyms for common words when they have the opportunity (e.g., car, automobile, vehicle).

Caregivers also have the opportunity to increase the types of conversations and vocabulary they would typically have with young children. This may include reading books that describe emotions, cultures around the world, and science concepts like an animal's habitat. The goal of exposing children to new vocabulary is not for the teacher to sound like a thesaurus, but instead, the caregiver can introduce children to new words so they are more likely to remember the word and its context the next time they hear them.

Children are not only learning new words when adults expose them to advanced vocabulary, but they are also learning how to use those new words in phrases and sentences (Bardige, 2016). They begin to learn the context of the new word and when it is appropriate to use it. Toddlers frequently test out how to use a new word by asking for something or repeating it both without and in context to see how an adult responds. They are also learning the sequence of words and how to tell a story using those words.

ROUTINE-BASED VERSUS PLAY-BASED LANGUAGE

There are many different routines in infant-toddler classrooms. Children experience routines with drop-off and pick-up, with mealtime, with diapering and toileting, and with sleeping. These are foundational parts of the day for infants and toddlers, and the caregiver must follow the needs of the child in order to set a daily schedule. Although the daily schedule for an infant-toddler classroom must be very flexible in order to include all of the children's daily routines, there should also be time dedicated to playing in the indoor and outdoor environments. During playtime, caregivers should be very purposeful in speaking to the children and interacting with them while they play on the floor of the classroom or on the slide in the playground. Language interaction during routines is just as essential.

These routine activities give infant and toddler caregivers a unique opportunity for one-on-one interaction with the child. While the caregiver is picking the child up to take him or her to the changing table or rocking chair, this is an opportune time to describe what is going on in the classroom or to tell the child what is going to happen next. When a caregiver is holding a child and giving him his bottle, it is the perfect opportunity to tell him that he is hungry and that he is drinking from his bottle so that he will not be hungry anymore. If the caregiver is holding a child to help her calm down, it is an opportunity to explain that she is sad but she is safe and loved.

These one-on-one language opportunities may not occur during playtime, even if the caregiver has planned special activities for the children. The caregiver may have to assist two or three children at a time, or plans may be changed. In the infant-toddler classroom the caregiver has to follow the needs of the children, and so planned activities may be rescheduled in order to assist with routine-based care. The best opportunity for a caregiver to interact individually with a child is during daily routines like feeding, diapering, and naptime, and so they must take advantage of this time.

SELF-TALK AND PARALLEL TALK

Research has established that children who hear more words are more likely to speak more words and understand the meaning of those words (Hart and Risley, 1995; Morgan et al., 2015). In an infant or toddler classroom where the children have limited verbal skills, it is essential that the caregivers speak to the children so that they can continually hear vocabulary and conversation. The adults become responsible for narrating what is happening in the classroom. They can do this in two ways: by describing their own actions in the classroom (self-talk) and by describing the experiences of the children and the other caregivers in the classroom (parallel talk).

By using these skills, the caregiver becomes the commentator on everything that is occurring in the classroom setting. This includes

- describing what he is seeing;
- describing what the child is seeing;
- describing what he is doing;
- describing what the baby is doing;
- asking a question and, after a pause, answering with the child's response;
- saying what he thinks the child wants to communicate;
- telling the child what is going to happen next;
- describing what the caregiver and the child are doing together;
- singing a song about what is happening in the classroom; and
- putting the child's feelings into words.

Even if the child is still nonverbal, it is important to always pause after making a statement or asking the child a question. If there is no pause, then the child never has the opportunity to be part of the conversation. When a child can contribute a response, it establishes the foundation for turn-taking in later conversations. The infant or toddler may also decide to respond with coos or gestures, and so it is important to give her the opportunity to do so. A caregiver also needs to make eye contact with the child when waiting for a response to show her that she is engaged in the conversation.

Babies provide a wide range of communication: smiles, worried looks, pointing, grasping, stiffening the body, tightening fists, and cuddling into the caregiver's body. It is important to acknowledge all of these types of communication as a contribution to the conversation and encourage the child to participate. When a toddler uses broken grammar to respond to the caregiver's statement, it is important to celebrate her response. When the caregiver responds back to the child, he or she can subtly correct the grammar in the statement and offer a positive model at that time.

SONGS, STORIES, AND FINGER PLAYS

Songs, stories, and finger plays contribute a large amount of language to the early childhood classroom. Even in a classroom of nonmobile infants, the caregiver has access to stories, songs, and finger plays to soothe the children, reinforce rhythm and steady beat, develop the focus, and increase vocabulary.

An infant's first contribution to "story time" is simply listening to the caregiver's voice say the words of the story. This is a familiar voice that already has the ability to begin soothing the child and helping her feel safe in the classroom environment. While the caregiver is reading the story, his tone of voice may rise or fall with the plot of the story. He will repeat new words that the child has never heard before and speak with a natural rhythm that is present in typical conversations. The child will initially learn to focus on the caregiver's voice, but as she hears words that she recognizes, she may begin to focus on repetitive words and how they are used.

An infant may respond to the story with coos or squeals, and a young toddler may repeat a single word that he has heard before. Older toddlers may begin to act out the actions of the story. By the age of two, most children can act out a story with more than one step, like putting a baby to bed or pretending to be a dog that barks (Bardige, 2016). Stories (especially nursery rhymes and fairy tales) tend to use a wider variety of vocabulary than people use in regular conversation, so children will hear a variety of words while listening to a short story. Since children then begin to imitate the language that they have heard, again and again, children who have been read to frequently begin to incorporate more advanced vocabulary into their own stories and pretend play (Bardige, 2016).

Finger plays accomplish many of the same skills as listening to stories, but they also focus on a rhythm pattern to the speech. Children may initially participate in finger plays by bouncing their bodies to the beat of the chant. They will eventually progress to speaking one-word phrases and then multiple words to the beat of the chant. The reinforced rhythm assists the child in developing the fluency that she will need in a typical conversation, as well as reinforcing steady beat. Finger plays further allow movement and coordination for the entire body and increase the child's fine motor development by isolating the movement of each individual finger. These simple chants can be implemented in the infant classroom long before the child can speak a word. The baby would simply need to listen and feel the movement as the caregiver bounces the baby up and down to the beat of the chant.

Finally, singing songs with young children can have an amazing impact on language development skills. Just like stories, songs usually have a larger range of vocabulary than used in typical conversations. When children are exposed to diverse vocabulary again and again through repetitive singing, they are more apt to understand the meaning of the words and later use them in phrases and sentences.

Another benefit of music is that setting words to a melodic tune increases the child's ability to remember those words. Caregivers have used this tool again and again to help students remember concepts like the letters of the alphabet, the capitals of all fifty states, and the past presidents of the United States. In infant and toddler classrooms, the caregivers are not trying to teach the children specific curriculum content. The benefit of using simple songs in the classroom is that children will hear a variety of vocabulary and be more apt to remember the words that they hear.

School readiness skills are built on the foundation of children's language abilities. Caregivers can begin to develop these language skills as early as the infant room. It is essential that infants and toddlers hear language throughout the day. They need to hear simple conversations and participate in responsive language interactions as soon as they can communicate with their families and caregivers. With daily and consistent language exposure, infants and toddlers will grow into kindergarten students who will be prepared to start reading and writing with the guidance of a supportive caregiver.

Chapter Four

Promoting Play Skills

Play is an essential part of early childhood. Maria Montessori (1948) defined "play" as the "work of the young child." Play is purposeful and enjoyable for young children, so they are drawn to it. It is their passion. The primary purpose of play is to explore the environment around them and learn through that exploration. By interacting with the people and the objects closest to them, young children learn how things work and what type of reactions they should expect.

Play affects the child's total development: cognition, social and emotional skills, physical development, and language skills (Ginsburg, 2007). Active play (e.g., crawling, running, and climbing) helps children to develop health habits and motor skills. Playing with other children increases language skills and helps them learn how to view the perspectives of others. Pretend play allows children to mimic adult behavior and eventually create their own behaviors. Play helps children develop self-regulation skills and begin to calm themselves independently when they become sad, frustrated, or angry (Bodrova and Leong, 2007). Playing in groups with adults or other children allows children to practice decision-making and learn how to be flexible. Although some of these skills sound advanced, caregivers begin establishing the foundation for each of these skills during infancy.

BENEFITS OF PLAY

Over the past decade, the American education system has begun to place a higher priority on academic skills in an attempt to help improve school readiness, instead of setting up classrooms to focus on play. As policies and trends have focused more on children sitting down at tables and chairs to memorize letters and count to ten, caregivers see the consequences of taking away necessary playtime. When children do not have ample playtime in the classroom, their social interactions are limited.

Children begin learning social rules in the infant classroom, like how to take turns speaking in a conversation. Free-choice playtime allows children to learn how to interact with one another, not just by using vocabulary but also by using proper social etiquette. Toddlers learn how to play beside one another without taking away a friend's toy or scratching a classmate. Without playtime, these rules are much harder to teach, since most children learn these through social play.

Playtime also gives children the opportunity to express their emotions in safe settings. Many toddlers use pretend play to imitate emotions they see their parents and caregivers demonstrate. When they enter preschool, they have the skills to demonstrate their own emotions in pretend play scenarios, instead of simply copying the behaviors of others. When we ask children to sit at a table and focus for long periods of time on academic skills, they do not have an outlet like pretend play to identify their own feelings. This leads children to internalize emotions and eventually to have large emotional outbursts when they cannot suppress these emotions any longer. More children are now starting kindergarten without the ability to calm themselves down when they become sad, frustrated, or angry, and this is putting these children at a disadvantage (Florez, 2011).

Active play allows children to develop more healthy habits, like moving through the classroom and seeking out information and materials. When children are asked to sit at desks at a young age, they begin to develop more sedentary lifestyle habits, like waiting for information to be brought to them. Adults are now counting their daily steps and forcing themselves to take the stairs instead of riding in elevators to avoid being overweight. Young children naturally want to move. Because they learn most effectively by using their senses, movement is a natural part of their development.

An appropriate classroom allows children to move around the room freely to discover new materials. Taking away this movement destroys some of the healthy habits that we hope all children will learn from a young age. Also, restricting a young child's movement can delay essential motor skills. When a caregiver keeps a child in a bouncy seat or an exersaucer for extended periods of time, that child is missing vital opportunities to learn to move. Children who fall behind developmentally with large muscle development to crawl, walk, run, jump, and climb will also struggle with small muscle movements later like holding a pencil correctly for writing letters or using scissors.

Without play-based early childhood classrooms it will be difficult for children to advance in the sciences. Play encourages children to observe the environment, to solve problems, and to use the scientific method to test out their plans for a possible solution. Simply playing in the block area with cars and using long blocks for inclined planes can lead to a hypothesis on why one car drives faster on one block compared to another. When children learn how to observe and make predictions at a young age, they are more likely to excel in the sciences later in school. Children that do not have an opportunity to explore and experiment may not develop this mindset.

Since play is such a necessary part of the early childhood classroom, caregivers have a large responsibility to make sure that all young children have access to playtime.

- Caregivers must understand the importance of play and incorporate it into their classrooms, starting in the infant room.
- Caregivers must be able to explain to parents why play is important and advocate for play as a large part of the daily classroom schedule, even explaining its impact on academic skills.
- Caregivers must set up their classroom environments so that infants and toddlers can engage in the earliest stages of play starting at the beginning of their childcare experience.

STAGES OF PLAY

In the 1920s, Mildred Parten, an American sociologist, began studying how young children play, individually and in groups. She was one of the first people to do extensive research on the benefits of play. Her research established that there are six distinct stages of play through which children move during childhood (Parten, 1932):

1. Unoccupied play—children play through unplanned exploration.
2. Solitary play—children select their own toys and materials and play near others. They still do not interact with others during playtime.
3. Onlooker play—children purposely watch others play, but they do not interact with them.
4. Parallel play—children play with similar materials in the same area as other children, but they are still not playing cooperatively with the other children.
5. Associative play—a group of children play in the same area with the same materials. They are interacting during their play, but they are not working toward a common goal.
6. Cooperative play—children play together with the same materials and have the same goal for their play.

The first four stages of play can be observed in the infant and toddler classrooms, and they set the foundation of higher-level play during the preschool and elementary school years. These stages focus on individual activities, but they are essential for children to play cooperatively later and to learn to be flexible and follow social rules.

Unoccupied play is an example of Piaget's concept of sensorimotor development (Parten, 1932). This stage typically includes children from birth to the age of two. Infants and young toddlers explore the environment through their senses. In order to learn, they need the opportunity to be a part of the environment. They want to touch it, taste it, see it, smell it, and hear it. Young children not only want to explore the environment and the toys around them, but they also want to explore the people in their environment. They want to hear their caregivers' voices and touch their faces.

During this stage of play development, caregivers need to set up the environment to encourage exploration.

- Classrooms need to have low shelves that small children can easily crawl or walk toward to obtain toys.
- Caregivers need to offer a variety of toys that children can choose from each day. These toys need to have a variety of textures and colors to help children take in as much sensory information as possible.
- Since children at this stage of play often place materials in their mouths to learn about them, caregivers need to have a system in place to clean toys effectively and return them to the shelves quickly so that more children can interact with them.
- When caregivers select toys, they need to think about all the sensory information that the material can offer the children. Infant and toddler classrooms need to provide toys that make sounds, light up, and react when a child pushes a button. The more input that children can receive through exploring the toy, the more the children's interests are piqued.
- In infant classrooms, the caregivers must set up the classroom with space on the floor for babies to lie on their bellies and observe the environment. Before infants are mobile, they still need floor time where the caregivers can provide toys within reach for them to explore.
- The classroom also needs to be set up for infants in a seated position to observe the room and gather information by watching others and listening to their voices.

The second stage of play is solitary play. This stage is more purposeful play, and it usually includes children in the age group of eighteen months to two and a half years (Parten, 1932). The children can maintain a small amount of focus on the activities they have selected. This stage of play is very functional. The children use the objects for their specific purposes instead of pretending the objects are something else. Children in this developmental stage are still very egocentric and focused on their own desires, so they are rarely interested in playing with or beside others. They can play in the same classroom as other children, but they will not show any cooperative skills.

The classroom caregivers can support children in this stage of development by

- offering duplicates of the most popular toys since children at this stage are not yet able to share;
- providing pretend play materials for children that are similar to items they see in their homes (since they are not yet able to adapt or create, only imitate adult behavior); and
- setting up the classroom with an area that allows toddlers to be alone if needed, since they are still focused on their own needs instead of on the needs of peers.

Onlooker play is when infants and toddlers begin to watch the play habits of others, even though they are not developmentally ready to play with other children yet (Parten, 1932). During this stage of play, children learn social interactions by watching adults interact with their peers. These children are typically between two and three years of age. They learn through watching children playing beside one another or with each other. When children are in a multiage infant and toddler classroom, younger children can benefit from watching toddlers in the beginning stages of parallel and associative play. During onlooker play, the child will sit or stand close enough to another child or a group of children in order to hear their interactions.

Caregivers can assist children in the onlooker play stage in the following ways:

- sitting on the floor and modeling how to use the toys in the classroom;
- using self-talk and parallel talk to model social interactions for the children in the classroom;
- positioning less mobile infants and toddlers in close proximity to their peers so that they may observe their play and interactions; and
- modeling play with a variety of different materials in the classroom and guiding more advanced toddlers to interact with different types of materials so that onlookers will view a variety of experiences.

The fourth stage of play is parallel play. This stage is the transition from individual activities to group activities (Parten, 1932). Children in this stage will often play with the same types of toys, in the same area of the classroom, but they are still playing individually. These children may be older toddlers or young preschoolers. They will frequently watch the other children in the area and will also mimic their actions. Parallel play will usually involve two to three children playing within close proximity of each other, but they still see the toys as their own property instead of shared materials. When the caregiver observes children in this stage of play, he or she will often see that the children show signs that they are willing to socialize, but they still do not possess the skills to create a social environment.

To support children in this stage of development, caregivers need to assist young children with the transition from individual to social interaction during play.

- Caregivers need to participate in play and model how to share materials and speak to the children during playtime.
- Caregivers need to assist children with sitting close enough to one another during parallel play that they can observe one another and model each other's behaviors.
- Caregivers should set up the classroom environment so that several centers are large enough for two or three children to have individual space in the same area.
- Caregivers also need to make sure that there are enough shared materials (like blocks) for several children to have their own individual portion.
- Since young children are learning how to play close to one another and still be peaceful, it is essential that children stay engaged in the toys and not constantly take toys away from one another. This means that caregivers must intentionally rotate toys in and out of the classroom so that children stay engaged with the materials on the shelves. When children are disengaged with the environment, they often look for engagement by beginning negative interactions with their peers.

When young children enter associative play, they have reached a milestone where they desire to interact with one another during playtime (Parten, 1932). This stage allows a group of children to participate in the same activity, but they are doing that activity individually. For example, three or four children may all be playing together in the dramatic play area of the classroom. One child is taking care of a baby. Another child is pretending to cook over the stove, and two other children are trying on dress-up clothes. They may have a conversation and ask the other children to look at what they are doing, but they are not working toward a common goal. There is not one plot for their play in the dramatic play area, but the children are enjoying telling one another about what they are each doing.

Associative play begins when children are older toddlers or preschoolers. This is when social skills significantly increase for young children, and because they are talking more, vocabulary also increases. Since children are now playing together, they begin forming friendships. As friendships are developing, children learn to negotiate and solve problems.

When children in this stage of play disagree, they often need an adult to moderate while they work out the problem. After they have watched an adult model these negotiation skills again and again, they begin to understand the process and try to solve the problem without adult assistance. Children also become much more interested in symbolic play (pretend play) at this stage because they now have the cognitive skills to pretend that one object is a symbol for another.

The following needs to be taken care of during the stage of associative play:

- Caregivers need to guide children who are arguing to express their feelings and listen to their peers' feelings. The adult may also need to suggest possible solutions to the argument and prompt the children to select a reasonable option.
- Caregivers need to set up the classroom environment with areas that focus on group play and symbolic play. This means that the block area, the dramatic play area, and the puppet stage need to have a wide variety of engaging materials to encourage children to play together and use symbolic play. It is also essential to provide symbolic play materials in the outdoor environment.

The final stage of play development is cooperative play. At this stage of play, children will play with the same materials in the same area with a common goal (Parten, 1932). This might mean that children are playing in the puppet area together with the goal of acting out the same story. Three or four children could all be sitting at the table together playing with play dough and making characters for the same story. Children at this level of development can start playing group games with simple rules. They are able to use symbolic play successfully. The children are usually in preschool or early elementary school and may be able to negotiate and solve problems without adult assistance.

Children in the cooperative play stage can engage in very advanced activities, so caregivers need to provide these children with opportunities to

- play simple board games;
- participate in games with simple rules like scavenger hunts, "Red Light, Green Light," or "I Spy";
- participate in group play like a doll house or puppet theater; and

- participate in small group activities like a science experiment where children work together to make predictions and follow directions (e.g., a sink-and-float experiment or a cooking activity).

Each child will move through the stages of play at a different rate, but the progression of the stages will stay the same for all young children. If a child has a developmental delay (such as a delay with social and emotional skills), then he or she is going to need more support from the caregivers to move through these developmental stages.

PRETEND PLAY

"Play" is a very broad term. It includes exploration, functional play (playing with objects for one specific purpose), constructive play (creating new things), outdoor play, individual play, cooperative play, and pretend play. Although play includes all of these different ways that children explore and interact with the people and the environment around them, pretend play (or symbolic play) is a specific type of play that is necessary for children's overall development and higher-level thinking skills.

Many families view pretend play as a recreational activity and not a learning experience. The truth is that pretend play skills have huge value. "Pretend play" can be defined as children acting out stories that involve the emotions and perspectives of different characters. Children use pretend play when manipulating dolls, when dressing up and pretending to be someone else, or by pretending to play with an imaginary person or character. Although these activities seem light-hearted, they have a powerful effect on multiple areas of development.

Pretend play allows children to play cooperatively, to share with one another, and to develop empathy for another person's situation. Young children typically see the world through their own eyes without considering the perspective of others. Pretend play opens the door for a child to consider how someone else feels and how a situation may affect more than one person. When children begin using pretend play skills, they are usually alone making toys interact with one another. As they become more advanced socially they begin to interact with other children and have more intricate pretend play plots. This often leads to more advanced problem-solving skills as children learn to solve a problem that another friend introduces to the pretend play scenario.

When caregivers listen to a child's language during pretend play, they may hear an exact replica of phrases and expressions that the child hears regularly from family members or caregivers. Pretend play encourages children to use language skills so that they can explain their actions and their stories to their peers. In group pretend play activities, the children must ask questions and explain themselves to further the story. Children also learn that language has meaning, which is a skill that will help with reading development.

When children are pretending, they often have a variety of problems to solve. They could be as simple as two children wanting to play with the same toy, or in a more advanced pretend play, they could have a mystery to solve and must move through stages of story development.

Pretend play also creates abstract thought. Children develop pretend play stories by seeing pictures in their minds and trying to act out those pictures with their bodies. If a child is missing a prop for his story, he must find a way to adapt the materials that are available and solve the problem. All of these skills lead to higher-level thinking.

Children often use both gross and fine motor skills in pretend play. These activities often encourage children to dress and undress in imaginative outfits, so children may be learning to snap, button, tie, and zip. These are all necessary self-help skills that assist with hand-eye coordination. Also, pretend play may encourage large muscle skills as well. When a child on the playground pretends to be a firefighter and climbs to the top of the play structure to save someone from a burning building, she is also working on climbing and visual discrimination.

In the infant and toddler classrooms, pretend play begins with a little girl walking around the classroom holding a purse from the dress-up area because she has seen her mother carry a purse. Another child may hold a pretend drill because he watched his grandfather use a drill to fix the deck last weekend. Toddlers may use small plastic people in the classroom dollhouse to move around the house or to observe what the people look like. They will not immediately begin using the people to have a conversation and tell a story like an older child could do. A toddler can begin moving the small replicas of the people around the house relating it to what his or her own home looks like. A toddler may hold a baby doll the same way that he observed his mother holding his baby sister at home. All of these skills are essential to developing more advanced pretend play skills later on in the child's development.

Infants and toddlers can begin to understand the emotions of others before they can identify those emotions with words. The pretend play materials in the classroom allow a young child to mimic these emotions. In a toddler classroom, a small child may pick up a doll and imitate a real baby crying. The caregiver can then interact with the toddler to use vocabulary like "I think the baby is upset." As young children mimic the emotions that they have watched in their daily lives, the caregiver can model the vocabulary to help children begin to identify these emotions. This process establishes a strong foundation for emotional health and self-regulation.

OUTDOOR PLAY

Although most play occurs indoors, it is essential for young children to experience outdoor play as well. Some caregivers may not offer infants and toddlers enough outdoor playtime because they are concerned about the temperature outdoors or about nonmobile children sitting on the ground. Despite these concerns, there are significant benefits for every young child to play outdoors, regardless of age (Council on Physical Education for Children, 2001). Caregivers can find age-appropriate ways to offer outdoor playtime to all children.

- Nonmobile infants can be taken outside in strollers or sit on a blanket on the playground.
- Toddlers can play on low playground equipment, go on short walks close to the childcare center, or go on stroller rides.
- During summer and winter weather, it is still essential to take young children outside; however, caregivers need to take precautions like wearing coats and mittens in the winter and wearing hats and sunscreen in the summer. Outdoor playtime may need to be reduced to avoid too much exposure to extreme temperatures, but most seasons will still allow for short trips outdoors.

Outdoor playtime improves overall health. A child's immune system is strengthened by some exposure to dirt and bacteria. Also, children receive additional vitamin D from outdoor playtime, which improves bone and dental health. Outdoor playtime allows children to exercise. Children develop endurance for longer amounts of active play and learn to lead more active lifestyles.

Outdoor play improves social and emotional development. Children engage in group play and simple games when they are playing outdoors. In the toddler classroom, a simple game may just be a game of chase, but it is still active, group play. Children learn to share materials with one another and negotiate when there is a disagreement.

Outdoor play improves gross and fine motor skills. Because large muscles in the body develop before small muscles, a child must learn to run and climb before doing more refined tasks. Outdoor play allows children to climb, swing, and run. Children develop balance, strength, coordination, and speed. Once a child has mastered these large muscle skills, then he or she will be more capable of holding a crayon or zipping a zipper when in the preschool classroom.

Outdoor play improves a child's concentration and focus. When children are indoors and sedentary for extended periods of time, they lose the ability to concentrate. When children have the opportunity to run and enjoy the outdoors, they frequently return to the classroom with a renewed ability to focus and complete a task.

Also, children who are allowed to explore the outdoor environment develop a stronger love for nature. These children frequently grow up learning to respect the environment and be good stewards of our natural resources. Outdoor play also improves children's mental health. It can improve a child's mood and reduce stress levels. It may also improve energy levels.

Young children in quality childcare programs should have daily opportunities to play outdoors. Sometimes caregivers do not take the children outside due to their own lack of energy or because they are not properly dressed for the weather. These obstacles do not benefit the children, and it is essential for all caregivers to advocate for outdoor playtime! Since children often become restless and unfocused without outdoor playtime, it benefits the caregivers and the students to utilize the outdoor environment each day.

Chapter Five

Physical Development of Infants and Toddlers

With regard to physical development, school readiness means that young children are ready to move through the environment—to explore and to interact with others. Once infants begin to move, they increase their ability to interact with the classroom, their peers, and their caregivers. Initially, their movement is limited. Younger infants can roll over to look at their classrooms from a different perspective or grasp the objects around them. As children become more mobile, they begin to explore more materials and take in more information.

The growing bodies of infants and toddlers achieve many gross motor milestones: crawling, walking, running, and climbing. As their large muscle skills become stronger, they begin to develop fine motor skills and can use their hands and fingers for more refined skills. These fine motor skills are an essential part of school readiness.

First, fine motor skills help young children to be more independent and learn to take care of themselves. Children begin to feed themselves by holding their own bottle or by using a spoon. As the children grow, they begin to undress and dress themselves, hold their own toothbrushes, and learn how to wash their own hands. Fine motor skills also prepare a child for the academic skills of kindergarten. As the muscles in children's hands and fingers become stronger, they develop the ability to hold and manipulate a crayon or a pencil. Most children are not prepared to draw shapes or letters until preschool; however, the toddler classroom prepares children for handwriting by allowing them to manipulate small objects with their hands and experiment with scribbling with crayons on paper.

Each child develops his or her physical skills at a different rate; however, children develop in a typical sequence. Physical development is cephalocaudal and proximodistal (Berk, 2012). "Cephalocaudal" means that young children develop from their heads down to their toes. Young infants first learn how to control their head movements. They develop muscles to lift and turn their heads, and then they begin to control their upper bodies. Finally, the children learn to use their legs and feet. By the age of twelve months, young children are attempting to take their first steps. Development is also proximodistal, meaning that children develop from their middle out to their extremities. This means that children learn to control their bodies' cores and their large muscle movements before learning to control their hands and feet that make more refined movements. If children do not gain control over their large muscle movements (sitting, crawling, walking, running, etc.), then it will be very challenging to refine fine motor skills like stringing beads or coloring with a crayon.

DEVELOPMENTAL MILESTONES

In order to assist children with their school readiness skills, it is essential that caregivers know the progression of developmental milestones for young children. Although it is appropriate to say that a skill like walking has a developmental milestone of twelve months, it is essential for caregivers to remember that each milestone actually has a window of time (before and after the milestone) that is considered appropriate for the skill (Berk, 2012). For example, children may start walking between ten months and sixteen months of age and still be on track developmentally. The milestone is just the average. Keeping in mind that each milestone has a window of time, here are the developmental milestones for physical development:

Two months
- can hold head up
- begins to push when lying on tummy
- arm and leg movements become more controlled

Four months
- holds head up steady, unsupported
- begins to push down with legs when feet are on hard surface
- may roll from tummy to back
- can hold toy and shake it
- can reach out to toys in line of sight
- brings hands to mouth
- when lying on tummy, can push up with elbows

Six months
- can roll over front to back and back to front
- begins sitting without support

- when supported in a standing position, can support weight on legs and possibly bounce
- can rock back and forth on all fours (may be starting to crawl backward)

Nine months
- can stand while holding on to something
- can get into a sitting position independently
- sits without support
- pulls up to stand
- crawls

One year (twelve months)
- gets into a sitting position independently
- pulls up to stand
- cruising (walks while holding on to furniture)
- can take a few unsupported steps
- can stand alone

Eighteen months
- walks independently
- may walk up steps
- may run
- pulls toys while walking
- drinks from a cup
- eats with a spoon
- assists with undressing

Two years (twenty-four months)
- runs
- kicks a ball forward
- stands on tiptoe
- climbs on and off of furniture without help
- leans over to pick up a toy without falling
- sits down in a small chair
- moves to music
- walks up and down stairs while holding on
- throws overhanded
- can copy or draw circles and straight lines

Thirty months
- jumps in place and falls when landing
- gallops
- threads large beads on a string
- copies a horizontal line

Three years (thirty-six months)
- climbs well
- runs well
- can pedal a three-wheeled tricycle
- walks up and down stairs rotating feet
- jumps with both feet together
- climbs up and down ladders
- scribbles with crayons
- may cut with scissors

SETTING UP THE ENVIRONMENT

Once the caregiver understands the developmental milestones for young children, he or she needs to *use* that information to create an environment that will allow the children to grow and develop in a safe place. A classroom environment that is set up based on the ages and ability levels of the children will allow them to explore and learn about the world around them. It will also keep them safe as they begin to move independently.

Some infant and toddler classrooms are set up for one specific age group, like a classroom of nonmobile infants. This type of classroom will be able to focus specifically on the abilities of nonmobile babies and provide materials only for infants. In a multiage classroom (infants and toddlers in the same classroom environment), the caregivers will need to make sure that the needs of all the children are met, despite the differences in age and ability. The benefit of a multiage setting is that nonmobile infants may be more motivated to begin crawling and eventually walking by watching their peers who are already moving independently throughout the classroom.

Young infants (under the age of six months) need to utilize a safe space on the floor of the classroom for tummy time (Sanders, 2015), so the caregiver must find a place in the classroom to lay down a soft blanket and allow the children to play on the floor. Caregivers can encourage the infants to stretch and balance by adding rattles and soft toys to the play environment. Infants will learn to reach and grasp when they see toys slightly out of their reach and are motivated to grab them.

Caregivers should move nonmobile infants to different locations in the classroom throughout the day to give them a different perspective on the room and what is going on among their peers. No baby should ever stay in the same position and the same location for more than thirty minutes. Caregivers need to make sure to stay close by and supervise tummy time. When young infants cannot control their neck movements, it is easy to rest their faces on the floor and block their mouths and noses. Once an infant becomes too tired to lift his or her head, then the caregiver needs to place the baby in a different position.

Children also need the opportunity during the day to be still and to have movement. Utilizing classroom materials like a bouncy seat may give a baby the extra movement she needs to stimulate the vestibular system and learn to feel her body moving through space. The infant also needs the opportunity to be still and rest her body.

Once young infants begin to be mobile (around six months of age), they need the opportunity to move around the classroom and develop their motor skills (Sanders, 2015). This means that the classroom safety features are even more important than when the infants were safe and secure in one location.

Once babies can explore the room, they begin placing everything in their mouths. Caregivers must make sure that there are toys on low shelves that are appropriate for infants to touch and taste. Once a child puts a toy in his mouth and then leaves it behind, the classroom must have a system for cleaning and sanitizing the toy before it is returned to the shelf. Infant toys must be small enough for an infant to grasp, but they must not be small enough for a child to choke on if placed inside his mouth. Supervision is still an essential part of the classroom. Even as caregivers work to meet the basic needs of the children in the classroom (feeding, diapering, etc.), they must closely watch the children moving around on the floor and exploring the classroom.

Caregivers also need to make sure that the room is set up for the youngest children to access. There should be small chairs and low shelves created for toddlers (Greenman, Stonehouse, and Schweikert, 2008). The caregiver needs to make sure that mobile infants and toddlers have the space to practice moving through the classroom. The furniture should be spaced far enough apart that a young child can push and pull toys through the room. The furniture should also allow enough space for adults to sit down on the floor and play with the children. Adults need to sit beside infants during tummy time, and they need to be on the floor to let toddlers sit in their laps to look at books. Caregivers need to sit with children at meals to model how to eat, and they need to play dress-up with children who are putting on hats in the dramatic play center. The classroom arrangement needs to support adult participation.

REFLEX MOVEMENTS

Newborn infants start their lives displaying motor skills. Many of these skills are reflexes, involuntary reactions to some type of stimulation. The reflex assists the baby with a response even before he or she has learned how to react to the stimulation. It is important for caregivers to learn about the purpose of these reflexes and how to stimulate the reflexes in order to be deliberate in assisting the infant with improving motor function (Sanders, 2015). The most common reflexes present in infants are the following:

- The rooting reflex—this reflex helps a baby find food. The caregiver can touch the baby's cheek beside the baby's mouth and he will begin to suck. This reflex is essential for survival.
- The sucking reflex—if a finger, nipple, or pacifier is placed into the infant's mouth, the infant will automatically begin to suck. Sucking helps infants find food, but it also helps with exploration and self-calming.
- The hand-to-mouth reflex—when the caregiver strokes the infant's cheek or the palm of her hand, the baby brings her hand to her mouth. Once the hand is close to her mouth, it can trigger the sucking reflex. The baby begins to identify her hands and fingers, and this will help her develop the arm strength to roll over.
- The tonic neck reflex—the caregiver can place a baby on his back and make a noise or speak to the infant. The baby will turn his head toward the sound and his arm on the same side will extend to the sound also. This reaction stimulates the vestibular system and moves the fluid in the baby's ears. These movements are strengthening the child's muscles to prepare to roll over in the near future.
- The grasping reflex—the caregiver touches the palm of the infant's hand, and the infant will grab the adult's finger and hold on tight. This is an involuntary response that strengthens muscle control. The reflex helps babies to hold on to people and objects.
- The step reflex—when the caregiver holds the baby up straight with hands under the infant's armpits and feet hanging and then lowers the infant's feet toward a hard surface, the infant will lift one foot and then another like she is taking steps. This reflex disappears after just a few months, but it does appear again around seven or eight months, when the baby is closer to being able to stand and then walk.
- The righting reflex—when the caregiver lays the infant on his back and gently covers his face with a light object (like a scarf), the infant will struggle and shake his head from side-to-side until his face is free. You can see this reflex when the baby is first learning to sit independently. If the baby falls over, his first instinct is to protect his face. He is born with the reflex to protect himself.

Several reflexes are linked to the infant's survival. Other reflexes lead to physical development in the months that follow. Repeating these reflexes with young children allows the muscles and skills to develop further and prepare for later mastery.

TRAVELING SKILLS (LOCOMOTOR MOVEMENTS)

Traveling skills help children get from one location to another (Sanders, 2015). They include rolling, crawling, walking, running, marching, galloping, skipping, and so on. Young children achieve many types of traveling skills during the first three years of life, so it is easy for the caregiver to assess their development. In order for children to develop traveling skills, the environment must allow them to have space to move throughout the classroom, and the classroom schedule must give children enough time each day to move and be physical. Young children master these traveling skills by repeating them over and over again. In order for the children to practice, the caregivers must make sure that there are no safety hazards (outstretched cords, clutter on the classroom floor, etc.) in the way of the children.

Tummy time is a child's first step toward traveling skills. Caregivers can begin using tummy time with infants around six weeks of age, but it is important to start with very small intervals of time. The caregiver needs to find a clean blanket to lie on the floor and then place the baby on his belly on top of the blanket. A six-week-old infant may only be strong enough to stay on his stomach for fifteen to thirty seconds before the caregiver needs to place him in a resting position. The caregiver needs to provide constant supervision when placing a baby on the floor on her stomach.

The caregiver can slowly lengthen the amount of tummy time as the child begins to develop muscle control over his head and neck. Some infants will struggle and cry a great deal when they are placed on their stomachs, but this activity will increase strength in the neck, upper back, arms, and legs. As the child's arms get stronger, he will eventually learn to push up and develop skills that will eventually help him crawl. By the time a baby is six months old, he or she can spend a combined total of ninety minutes of tummy time throughout the day (Sanders, 2015). Once infants are strong enough to begin scooting or crawling around the room, then traveling skills begin.

Children begin to travel around the classroom when they are interested in everything they see, hear, smell, touch, and taste. Children are motivated to crawl, walk, or run when they are interested in the environment around them. The environment must make exploration possible. The classroom toys need to be on low shelves for the children to reach, and the classroom needs to provide open space for the infants and toddlers to move around. Adults need to be close by to assist children who are still unstable and can't move independently yet.

Caregivers need to encourage children to move and try new skills. It is important for adults to model the skill that the children are working on and engage in play with the children while they practice. The caregiver can get down to eye level and encourage an infant to crawl forward, or she can hold the hands of a new walker as the infant takes his first steps. The caregiver can also create challenges for children while they are practicing a skill, like creating a small obstacle course in the classroom for a child to crawl through.

Traveling skills go through a predictable pattern: crawling, walking, running, and so on. It is important for caregivers to encourage children to move through this pattern in the correct progression. Adults may get excited when an infant begins to walk before learning to crawl; however, when these skills are learned out of sequence, the child may not have full control of his or her movements, because essential muscles were not properly developed.

Children need to have both active time and rest time during the classroom schedule, so that their bodies have time to recover after practicing so many motor skills. Infants need to experience tummy time several times each day. All young children, both infants and toddlers, need to have outdoor time at least twice a day. This can include stroller rides, sitting in the grass, swinging, and playing on the playground.

The outdoor environment is an additional motivation for young children to move and explore the world around them. It is also important for infant and toddler classrooms to have age-appropriate materials and toys. This can include blankets with different textures, toys for chewing, mirrors, push and pull toys, indoor climbing toys, low chairs, appropriately sized playground equipment, and low shelving that does not encourage young children to climb to high locations.

STRENGTH AND BALANCE SKILLS

Balance skills allow children to move safely and control their body movements (Sanders, 2015). These skills include rolling, standing, turning, swinging, stretching, and bending. Strength skills assist children with balance and give them the power to move around their environment. Caregivers initially provide strength to support infants' bodies as they cradle babies in their arms. As older infants and toddlers develop strength, they have the ability to support themselves.

Balance skills relate back to the vestibular system. This system controls the body's ability to balance. It is located in the inner ear, the same location where children hear sounds. Fluid in the inner ear moves back and forth to help children know where their bodies are and then sends those messages to the brain (Sanders, 2015). The vestibular system allows children to feel where their bodies are in space.

Children experience two different types of balance as they master these skills. During static balance, a child holds his or her body in a position while not moving. This involves holding the muscles still and not falling over. During dynamic balance the child has control of his or her body while moving. Dynamic balance also includes balance during starting and stopping (Sanders, 2015).

Nonmobile infants learn balance skills when caregivers place them in an off-balance position and allow the baby to correct his or her own balance. For example, if the caregiver lays the infant down on the floor on his or her side, the baby may correct the position by rolling over onto his or her back. There are many types of activities that caregivers can do with infants in the classroom to help them develop balance skills:

- floor play on activity gyms that allows babies to reach for hanging toys;
- playing movement games where the baby lays down on the floor on his back and the caregiver moves the infant's arms and legs to cross midline;
- assisting the baby with bicycle kicks while lying on the floor;
- holding the baby in different positions that will put him slightly off balance and make him tighten muscles to feel secure again; and
- arm pull-ups where the caregiver lays the baby on her back and allows her to grab the caregiver's fingers as the latter slowly pulls her top half off of the floor and moves the center of gravity.

As infants become mobile (six to twelve months of age), their strength and balance skills increase a great deal. When babies start crawling, there is a greater amount of support, because the baby has a greater base for the center of gravity when crawling on all fours. Older infants are much less stable as they progress to standing and walking. Activities for mobile infants include

- bouncing lap games;
- baby arm pull-ups to a sitting position;
- swinging;
- baby wheelbarrow walking;
- assisted walking (while the infant holds the caregiver's fingers for support);
- chasing games (crawling or walking); and
- baby's first obstacle course.

Toddlers frequently learn balancing skills by demonstration. They are independently mobile and very interested in observing their peers and their caregivers. Caregivers can create games to encourage toddlers to test their strength and balance skills. Outdoor play on gross motor equipment will also help children learn to balance and climb. Activities for toddlers include the following:

- balancing bean bags (This may start with body-part identification and asking the toddler to hold the bean bag against his or her knee, elbow, head, etc.);
- simple balance beams (This could begin with walking on tape laid down on the floor and progress toward walking on a beam on the playground.);
- jumping games (both feet, then one foot at a time);
- riding push toys and then riding tricycles; and
- older toddlers will begin to navigate balancing and climbing on more advanced playground equipment.

MANIPULATION SKILLS

Manipulation skills can be defined as large motor or fine motor skills. The hand and arm muscles manipulate smaller toys and tools like rattles, puzzles, crayons, or even balls. This all starts when the infant learns to grasp. Manipulation skills include throwing, catching, kicking, striking with body parts, and striking with tools.

Infants learn to grasp as they first explore the environment. When they start to grasp, they have little control over the object they are holding. Their movements may be jerky, and they may accidentally drop their toys as quickly as they obtain them. For greatest success, the objects must fit easily into their hands. As fine motor skills increase, children can manipulate both small and large objects, using the whole hand or a few fingers working together.

One of every child's favorite toys is a ball. Playing with balls requires traveling skills and manipulation skills. Balls for toddlers must be lightweight and of the appropriate size. Toddlers can learn to throw and catch with two hands with larger balls. The ball must be smaller to teach one-handed throwing. The best materials for learning to throw and catch are bean bags, beach balls, plastic balls, and rubber balls. Scarves and bubbles are also good for learning catching skills. No ball should be small enough for a toddler to swallow and choke on. Playing with balls is very open-ended and creative. Children do not need specific instructions to stay interested.

Rolling is the first skill a child will learn. Children learn concepts like speed, effort, and direction when rolling a ball. Toddler will learn about kicking by watching someone demonstrate it. At first, he may barely make contact with the ball. Once he begins to make consistent contact with the ball, then he will learn about kicking with speed or kicking with force. Finally, he may be able to kick with direction. Most toddlers will wait for the ball to stop before kicking it.

Toddlers will eventually learn how to throw balls. This begins by simply dropping the same object over and over again. As the child gains more skill, he or she will eventually learn to bounce, throw underhanded, and then throw overhanded (eighteen months or older). Then toddlers will move to catching. First they catch with the entire body (like catching a beach ball), and eventually they will catch using just the arms and then hands.

The use of musical tools also involves locomotor skills and manipulation skills. Using instruments and dancing to music will introduce interlimb coordination (i.e., the hands and feet working together). Children first learn to clap and eventually learn to clap with a steady beat. Once the toddlers are interested in the music, they often begin by moving scarves or ribbons around the room. Caregivers can introduce rhythm sticks. Children can explore the rhythm sticks by drumming on the floor and hitting them together. As the toddler becomes more aware of the music's beat and pattern, he or she may make coordinated movements with the rhythm sticks. When the children explore different types of instruments like drums, tambourines, and shakers, they are required to manipulate the instruments using different methods.

TRACKING SKILLS (VISUAL DEVELOPMENT)

Visual development allows the child to follow the movements of the eyes, and the ocular system is responsible for these tracking skills (Sanders, 2015). During the first two years of life, the children learn to maintain visual contact with an object. They learn to look into the eyes of their caregivers when they are talking, and they can watch their peers move across the room. The visual system is not fully developed at birth. Children must practice watching others and repeat those experiences to develop their eyesight fully.

When children use their visual skills to track objects, they can learn the size, shape, and color of the objects. They can also learn that these concrete characteristics do not change as the object moves. Tracking skills develop when the infant is approximately three months old and begins to visually follow objects. The infant may develop 20/20 vision by the time he or she is eight months old. At one year of age, the infant can judge distance between objects and more spatial relationships. Caregivers can use the following activities in order to assist infants with developing tracking skills:

Activities for zero to six months
- Talk to the baby as you walk around the room, allowing the infant to follow your voice
- Hang a mobile in the crib
- Rotate the left and right sides when you feed the baby to give a different visual perspective

- As the infant learns to grasp, move toys back and forth to give the baby a different perspective on what the toy looks like
- Daily tummy time
- Provide the infant with colorful toys that attract his or her attention

Activities for six to twelve months
- Encourage crawling before walking for better hand-eye coordination
- Allow the infant to pick up objects in a basket or small container and then dump them out again and again
- Hand clapping games like Pat-a-cake
- Hide and seek games (hiding a toy or a person's face behind a blanket)
- Blowing bubbles

Once infants have the ability to track objects and follow their movement, they begin to develop hand-eye coordination. This is the young child's ability to guide the hands in their movements. Hand-eye coordination helps toddlers to begin to develop physical skills. It contributes to fine motor development, also handwriting and reading skills. Activities for hand-eye coordination and fine motor skills include

- flashlight games;
- blowing bubbles;
- introducing balls and rolling games;
- beginning self-help skills like self-feeding, brushing teeth, getting undressed and dressed;
- large bead stringing;
- stacking blocks; and
- beginning scribbling with crayons.

When young children have the opportunity to develop their traveling skills, strength and balance skills, manipulation skills, and tracking skills, they will be more prepared for the expectations of school. The caregivers in the infant and toddler classrooms must create an environment that motivates children to move and then participate with other children in the environment to support them as they meet each milestone for their ages and abilities.

Chapter Six

Developing Self-Help Skills

When children begin kindergarten, it is essential that they be able to independently take care of their basic care needs. This includes skills like grooming, feeding, toileting, dressing, and self-regulation. These are often called self-help skills. Although self-help skills do not look like typical kindergarten academic skills, they are important. If a child comes to kindergarten and is unable to snap his pants after using the restroom or calm himself down after getting upset, then the teacher must stop what he or she is doing to help that child. When the teacher must stop teaching in order to assist a child with a self-help skill, the whole classroom loses teaching time. In order to move ahead with kindergarten academic skills, the children in the kindergarten classroom must be able to take care of their own basic care needs.

Although some self-help skills are more advanced, like zipping a coat or tying shoes, many of these skills are introduced in the infant or toddler classroom. Initially, when new skills are introduced, the caregiver is guiding the child through the process. For example, when a baby cries, the caregiver helps soothe her so that she will stop crying. Eventually, the baby becomes more independent. She may be able to soothe herself occasionally by using a pacifier or by becoming interested in other objects around the room.

Although a toddler cannot dress himself yet, he is introduced to this concept by simply assisting the caregiver while she dresses or undresses him. This could mean that the child does not fight the caregiver while she changes his clothes. A more practiced toddler may even assist the caregiver by raising his arms up in the air while the caregiver takes off his shirt. When a caregiver allows the child to have small amounts of independence in the infant and toddler classroom, then the child is more likely to become independent in the preschool classroom.

A large portion of a child's success with self-help skills is how confident he feels in the classroom and with the new skill. It is essential for caregivers to offer young children the opportunity to be independent and to set up the classroom for children to make independent choices. When a child is courageous enough to try something new, it is important for the caregiver to offer praise and recognition. This type of verbal encouragement increases the child's self-esteem, and she will be more apt to try something new again in the future.

DEVELOPMENTAL MILESTONES

In order to assist young children with self-help skills, caregivers need to know what the children are capable of doing. This means that each caregiver must learn the developmental milestones for self-help skills, as well as the other areas of development:

Six months
- bring bottle to mouth independently

Nine months
- hold the handle of a spoon
- pick up small finger foods

Twelve months
- begin to drink from a cup
- bring spoon to mouth for feeding
- give familiar toy to an adult by request
- come when requested

Fifteen months
- assist when an adult is helping with undressing and dressing
- pull socks off
- feed self with a spoon (with some spilling)
- understand some simple routines and possibly participate in them

Eighteen months
- take off shoes
- make choices and use the word "No"
- assist with simple tasks like cleaning up toys
- recognize the parts of the body and point to them
- hold a small cup with one hand

Two years
- wash hands
- pull pants down and up without help (with an elastic waistband)

- work on toilet training
- undress

Thirty months
- dress with some assistance
- use a fork
- enjoy independence

Three years
- put on socks and shoes (may need assistance with Velcro)
- brush hair
- brush teeth

It is always important to remember that each child develops at a different rate, so some children may be ahead of these milestones, while others may need additional time to reach a goal. With many self-help skills, children will not be able to meet these goals if they are not given the opportunity to practice (Sandall and Schwartz, 2008). For example, a child will not be able to meet the milestone of completing simple tasks like cleaning up toys if the caregiver consistently does this task for her. In order to meet the goal, the child must have practice.

It is not unusual for caregivers to continue to feed a child even after he has the ability to feed himself. This might happen because the caregiver is in a hurry or because the caregiver does not want to clean up the mess that occurs when the child feeds himself. However, the child will continue to be messy and take a long time to self-feed if he does not have practice.

SELF-REGULATION

Self-regulation is the ability to monitor and control our own behavior and emotions based on the situation at hand (Cook and Cook, 2010). This includes controlling impulsive reactions, ignoring irrelevant information, and focusing on the current task even if it isn't as enjoyable as others. To be successful in school, children need to learn how to regulate their emotions in social situations and even their attention and focus. Children who learn to self-regulate successfully are able to

- verbally communicate their needs, wants, and thoughts to teachers and peers;
- devote their attention to a task until completion;
- show curiosity and enthusiasm about new activities;
- reduce impulsive behavior (think before acting);

- follow two-step and three-step directions;
- share and take turns with peers; and
- be sensitive to other people's feelings.

As children are exposed to academic learning at younger ages, there seems to be a growing number of children entering kindergarten that are struggling with self-regulation. Early childhood caregivers have a growing responsibility to assist children in their care with developing these social and emotional skills at a young age to prepare them best for successful school experiences in kindergarten and throughout their formal education.

First, a high-quality early childhood education, beginning in the infant and toddler classroom, can help to establish a secure emotional foundation between the caregiver and the child. Once that secure foundation is established, children are more likely to be curious learners and explore the classroom, but they must know that they have a safe place to return to when they are scared or frustrated. Once the secure relationship is in place, children are more likely to interact with classroom peers. Those interactions will help them learn about the social rules of the classroom and the emotions of others.

When the early childhood classroom begins to focus on academic skills at too young an age, before relationships have been established or before the child is able to focus on an activity, children will show higher levels of emotional distress and will not understand how to handle those emotions. The best learning environments offer strong relationships and a classroom setup for the children to explore at their own pace. This means that the caregiver does not force the child to make a choice or to spend a specific amount of time using that material. The child is led by his level of interest, and as he matures, his level of interest will become longer and more focused. Once he has the ability to focus, he will not become frustrated. Instead, he will feel successful.

The infant and toddler classroom must be set up so that young children can explore. There should be low shelves with toys that are appropriate for young children. Toddlers should be able to walk up to the shelf and select their own toys. This also allows children to move from activity to activity at their own discretion. This level of independence allows them to feel successful.

There are three steps that will help young children significantly when it comes to learning to regulate their own emotions and focus: modeling, offering additional cues and hints, and withdrawing adult support as the students succeed (Florez, 2011). The caregivers should be sitting on the floor with the children and modeling how to use the toys. This gives young children an example without forcing them to select a certain toy. Caregivers also need to model how to behave when something goes wrong. This demonstrates to the children how the caregiver controls her emotions.

Along with modeling, caregivers also need to offer simple cues or hints to help the children (Florez, 2011). This might include the caregiver offering the child simple directions (e.g., use your gentle hands), or it could mean that the caregiver rubs the child's back as he is getting upset to help him calm down. Some children need to see modeling and have additional help in order to control their emotions. The caregiver needs to understand the temperament of the child to know how much additional support he will need.

Once a child becomes more independent at controlling her emotions, then the caregiver should gradually withdraw extra support (Florez, 2011). Infants and toddlers may need high levels of support when they are first learning to interact with others, but as they have small successes, it benefits them if some of the caregiver's support is withdrawn so that they can feel successful and independent. These successes will motivate the children to be independent again in the future.

FEEDING

As soon as the child is able, the caregiver should encourage her to begin participating in the feeding process. For an infant, this may mean that the baby grasps the bottle as the caregiver provides it to her. Once the infant is sitting up and grasping, the caregiver can let her hold her own spoon, even if the adult still does most of the feeding. When the infant is introduced to more solid foods, the caregiver needs to cut up the food into bite-sized pieces and allow the child to grasp each piece and bring it to her mouth. This can be a time-consuming and messy process; however, it is an essential step for the infant.

Many families may be apprehensive about letting an infant or young toddler begin feeding himself. The family could be scared of the child choking, or they may enjoy the time spent together when the adult is feeding the baby. If the family is not yet ready to allow the infant to self-feed, it is important to go over the safety precautions that need to be in place.

For example, when an infant begins to hold her own bottle, it is still important for the caregiver to hold the baby during feedings to make sure that the baby does not choke and can stop the flow of the milk when she is ready to stop eating. Once the baby is eating soft foods, it is important for the infant to be sitting up straight and alert so that he does not choke. When finger foods are introduced, it is very important to begin with soft foods that are easy to swallow. It is also important to give a toddler-sized portion of food and to cut each item into very small bites. A young toddler should never be left alone while eating.

Family style meals allow toddlers to feel independent, but they also include the safety features and the bonding time that children received when they were fed one-on-one as an infant. In the classroom, family style dining begins with having small chairs and tables that allow the children to sit at the table and still have their feet on the floor for stability. Children are also offered child-sized cups and plates for their food and drink. Toddlers should also be offered spoons (and forks as they become more accomplished). There should be a combination of finger foods and foods the children can eat with a spoon. Although this can lead to very messy mealtimes, it does allow the children to feel a sense of accomplishment.

Before children sit down at the table, they should be guided to wash their hands. Once they are seated at the table, the adult should assist the children with the serving spoon and placing food on the plate. This helps children see an appropriate portion and learn to use the serving utensils. Initially the caregivers may need to pour the milk, but as soon as the toddler is able to assist, he should be included in the process. This can begin by having the toddler hold the cup with two hands while the adult pours.

Eventually the child will be able to help hold the handle while the adult pours. Young toddlers will probably use cups with lids, or sippy cups, when first eating at the table. By the age of two, the children should be able to use a small cup with an open mouth. It is important to remind toddlers gently that they should drink while sitting down at the table and not while wandering around the classroom.

Once the food is served, the caregiver should sit down at the table to eat and model the appropriate table etiquette. During the meal, it is important to encourage the children to participate in conversation. This is the equivalent to the caregiver holding the infant in her arms and singing to her while she gives her a bottle. The caregiver should ask the children questions about the meal, about what they have been playing with, and about how they feel. Children will naturally eat their meal at an appropriate pace if they have the opportunity to pause and engage in conversation.

Caregivers should never force a child to eat or tell them that they must eat more of one food if they wish to have more of another. It is important for young children to learn when they feel full after a meal, and they are more likely to overeat if they are required to eat certain items on their plates. Toddlers are not growing as rapidly as infants, so their meal patterns may change slightly. They are more likely to eat only at mealtimes and a few planned snacks, compared with infants, who are fed on a much more rigorous schedule.

When toddlers finish eating at a family style meal, they should also help with the cleanup process. Young toddlers may only be able to throw away their napkins and assist with handwashing after the meal. As the toddlers become more independent, they can also throw away their remaining food and place their cups and plates in the dirty dish pile.

DRESSING

Even though young children will not be able to dress themselves successfully until they are three years old or older, many of the skills needed for dressing begin in the infant and toddler classroom. The first step toward dressing is when a young infant stops fighting her caregiver during a clothing change and allows the caregiver to change her clothes without resistance. Also, during infancy, caregivers are frequently pointing to parts of the child's body and labeling them out loud (e.g., "tummy, toes, leg"). This process is extremely important when teaching young children to dress and undress themselves.

Infants and toddlers need to know the names of the parts of their bodies before they can begin assisting the caregiver with dressing. Once the child knows how to identify his head and his arm, then he is able to assist the caregiver when she says, "I am putting the shirt over your head." After the children know the parts of their body, then they begin to assist the caregiver with dressing.

Toddlers begin to undress themselves independently between sixteen and twenty-four months of age. Undressing is usually easier than dressing because the children just have to pull off pieces of clothing, instead of manipulating parts of their bodies into the clothing when dressing. Children usually begin kicking off their shoes first. Once a child is able to take off her shoes successfully, then she will pull off her socks, her hat, or a hair bow. Finally, she learns to take off her shirt and her pants. Many young children will learn how to take off their diapers before they are toilet trained, and this can be especially problematic at nighttime.

Once a child is around two years old, he can begin to put clothing on himself. This is typically the time period during which caregivers ask the family to avoid clothing with buttons and snaps or overalls. It is much easier for a child to learn to dress himself with elastic waistband pants. At the age of two, the child may also be ready to start toilet training, and he will be much more successful if he can quickly pull his pants down before sitting on the toilet. Clothing that allows the child to be more independent will also help eliminate more toileting accidents.

Older toddlers may begin to show interest in the dramatic play area of the classroom. This allows the children to practice putting on clothing with many different fasteners like Velcro, zippers, buttons, and laces. As the children practice dressing and undressing in the pretend clothing, they will become more accomplished at working with their own clothing. Young children should begin with using Velcro openers first. A child will not be able to learn to tie shoes until the age of five or six, so it is best to have Velcro fastened shoes at this age.

It is also important to make a toddler responsible for her own coat. This process can begin by making the child retrieve her coat when it is time to go outside or to go home. As she becomes more accomplished, then she may be able to put her arms in the coat correctly. Then the caregiver can zip the coat for her after she has begun the process.

GROOMING

Children learn many of their grooming habits when they are in elementary school and become independent enough to shower on their own or fix their own hair in the morning. Young children can also learn basic grooming skills, even in the infant classroom. As soon as babies are able to stand independently, the caregiver begins introducing them to handwashing at the sink.

Since handwashing is important to keeping the children and the caregivers in the classroom healthy, it is the first grooming skill that is introduced. The caregiver initially teaches handwashing in a hand-over-hand method where the caregiver turns on the water, places the infant's hands in the water, puts the soap on the infant's hands, rubs the hands together, rinses the hands in the water, and then dries the hands off with a paper towel. The child is learning the steps of the routine with the caregiver carrying out the steps. This should be done at a sink that is within comfortable reach of the child. The child can stand on a secure step, but he should still be secure throughout the handwashing process. As the child gains more independence, the caregiver can let him complete certain steps on his own (e.g., rubs his hands together and makes bubbles).

By the time the child is two years old, he should be able to complete this process independently, includes turning off the water and throwing away his paper towel. Once children are able to wash their hands independently, the caregiver still will need to remind them when it is appropriate to wash their hands. Children may often need a reminder after coughing, sneezing, or playing outside. If the caregiver consistently offers reminders to the children throughout the day about when they should wash hands, then the children begin to learn the routine and become more independent. Caregivers will still need to give children some general guidance like using one finger to test the temperature of the water before placing both hands completely into the water.

Another important grooming skill for the toddler classroom is learning how to blow noses. When a toddler has a runny nose, it is helpful for the caregiver to show her in the mirror that her nose is runny. Then, while still standing in the mirror, show the child how to use the tissue to wipe the nose and pull the tissue away from her face. This lesson concludes with showing the child how to throw away her tissue and wash her hands.

Once a child is successful at wiping a messy nose, the caregiver can model for the child how to blow her nose. This is a more advanced skill, and some children will not master it until preschool. Many children naturally sniff in air when they are shown how to blow air out of their nose. Again, it is important to demonstrate throwing the tissue away and washing hands afterward. When a caregiver has children in the classroom that are learning to wipe and blow their noses, it is very important to keep tissues out where the children can reach them independently.

Many toddler classrooms begin teaching children how to brush their teeth. Children are typically four years old or older before they are independent with tooth brushing, and many pediatric dentists will advise families to continue brushing the child's teeth until kindergarten to make sure that all of the teeth are getting clean. Even still, it is important for toddlers to get into the habit of taking care of their teeth and being comfortable with the feeling of the toothbrush in their mouths.

The caregiver needs to provide each child with a child-sized toothbrush with soft bristles. The caregiver will initially place a small amount of toothpaste on the toothbrush (about the size of a pea) and then help the child move the toothbrush around the mouth in small circles. This is a good time to sing a song like "The Alphabet Song" and teach the children the appropriate length of time to keep brushing. Afterward, it is important to show the children how to spit the leftover toothpaste into the sink, because some children are more likely to swallow it.

TOILETING

Toilet training a toddler is based not only on the toddler's self-help skills, but also on the temperament of the toddler. Many families would like to start the toilet training process early in order to stop changing dirty diapers and to stop spending additional money on diapers and wipes. Unfortunately, attempting to toilet train a child before the child is ready usually leads to further delays in toileting. Here are a few signs that children are ready to begin toilet training:

- They show interest in using the toilet.
- They begin waking up from sleep with a dry diaper.
- They use the words *potty*, *pee*, or *poopoo* and understand their meaning.
- They can pull their pants up and down independently.
- They can wash their hands independently.
- They have a predictable pattern each day for when they go to the bathroom.
- They want their diapers changed as soon as they are wet or soiled.

Although a child may start toilet training at two years old, many children will not be completely toilet trained until three and a half or even four years old. The process can take a long time. Some children may resist being toilet trained when they perceive that they are being told what to do and are not offered any independence (Gonzalez-Mena, 2014). If a child feels forced into the process, then he may refuse to use the toilet at all. This can often lead to delays in toilet training or even severe constipation. Caregivers must follow the lead of the child during this process and offer the child as much independence as possible in order to be successful.

The toilet training process should begin around eighteen months when the child and the caregiver have casual conversations about the toilet. The caregiver should allow the child to look at the toilet and even flush it. In order for the child to be most successful, the toilet should be child-sized so that the child can touch the floor securely and there is a ninety-degree angle between the child's feet, knees, and lap. That will allow the child to feel secure when sitting down on the toilet.

If the child has a consistent elimination pattern, then the caregiver should encourage the child to sit on the toilet at the time of day that the child usually goes to the bathroom. This should not be forced. The caregiver needs to offer the children praise for sitting on the toilet and trying and offer praise for successfully using the toilet; however, the caregiver should not offer rewards for using the toilet.

Once the child has started to use the toilet regularly, the caregiver should anticipate accidents. Families should provide several additional changes of clothing each day and anticipate taking home some wet and soiled garments.

It is important for the caregivers to help the children learn to wipe themselves after using the restroom. This means teaching the children how much toilet paper is necessary and to wipe from front to back. Disposable training pants, like pull-Ups, still feel like diapers to most children, so when a child is ready to try going to the toilet regularly, it is important to make the switch to cloth underpants. If the family tries cloth underpants and the child is having frequent accidents, then it may be time to go back to diapers for a while and try underpants again in a month or two when the child is more mature in order to have a positive experience.

SUPPORTING SELF-HELP SKILLS

The first step to helping children achieve independence in self-help skills is to make sure that they are included in daily classroom routines.

- Whenever possible, the caregiver needs to offer toddlers simple choices so that they feel independent.

Developing Self-Help Skills

- Caregivers need to celebrate the children's successes with handwashing, cleaning up a toy, using a cup without slipping, or using the toilet.
- When introducing new skills like sitting at the table to eat or cleaning up toys, the caregiver needs to model the behavior that he or she wants the children to demonstrate.
- Caregivers need to teach children the steps of important classroom self-help skills like get tissue, blow nose, throw tissue away, and wash hands. Young children may need verbal reminders, or the caregiver can use a picture schedule so that the children can physically see the steps they need to follow.
- The caregiver may need to use hand-over-hand assistance with the youngest children when introducing new skills, like how to use a spoon.
- The caregiver can make these self-help skills entertaining by teaching the children a fun song or dance to help them through the activity.

As the children grow, they will typically desire more independence, so they are naturally curious about how to do these activities. If a child has a developmental delay, like a motor delay, then self-help skills are naturally going to be more difficult and will take more practice in order to be independent. Remember that each child develops at a different pace, and caregivers need to offer help to support children who are not yet independent.

Chapter Seven

Cognitive Development and Pre-Academic Skills

Discussion on cognitive development of young children often leads to thoughts of learning to read and write. Although academic skills are included in the cognitive domain of development, there are many skills that begin long before a kindergarten student learns to write his name and memorize the letter sounds. The brain begins to develop before the child is born, and at birth, the child already has almost all of the neurons that she will ever have (Nowakowski, 2006).

The brain doubles in size during the first year of life, and by the age of three, the brain is already 80 percent of the size it will be when the child is an adult. That means that 80 percent of brain growth occurs while the child is an infant and a toddler. Another important fact is that synapses (the pathway between neurons that allow the neurons to communicate) are formed at a faster rate during the infant and toddler years compared to any other time in life. By age two or three, the brain has twice as many synapses as it will have in adulthood, since the brain later prunes (or removes) those synapses that are not being used. If the infant and toddler brain is growing at this rate, then it is essential that the child be in an environment that allows her to soak up knowledge and reach the brain's full potential.

Babies are born ready to learn. They can recognize their parents' voices within one week after birth because they have heard those voices over and over again in the womb. They are also born ready to recognize human voices over other sounds, and they are able to identify the smell of their own mother's milk. Their brains are created to learn and take in new information right from the beginning of life.

PIAGET'S THEORY ON CHILD DEVELOPMENT

Jean Piaget was a Swiss psychologist that lived from 1896 to 1980, and he is predominantly known for his theory on the stages of development. Piaget (1952) believed that there are four stages of intellectual development that each individual moves through in his or her lifetime: sensorimotor development, preoperational development, concrete operations, and formal operations. The first stage of development, sensorimotor development, lasts from birth to approximately two years of age. During this time period, children learn by taking information in through their senses. They absorb information when they get to touch, taste, see, hear, and smell the environment around them.

During sensorimotor development, children are initially aware of what happens immediately in front of them. When an infant is only three or four months old, she begins to imitate others (Piaget, 1952). When a caregiver speaks to the infant, she may attempt to make a similar sound in return. The baby begins to realize the difference between the environment and herself. As the infant ages, she begins to realize that objects and people still exist even when she cannot see them. This is called object permanence. Once a baby becomes mobile and can crawl around and explore the environment, cognitive development begins to increase. Now the child can explore and take in information from the entire environment, instead of what is within her reach when she sits up.

The second stage of development is the preoperational stage. This begins around the age of two, but each child reaches this stage at his or her own pace. This is the stage of development when a child can first use symbolic thought (Piaget, 1952). The child's language skills grow at a rapid rate from the onset of the preoperational phase. Children also develop their memory and imagination skills. This stage lasts through the age of seven, but you can already see each of these skills emerge in older toddlers.

DEVELOPMENTAL MILESTONES

So much cognitive growth occurs during the first three years of life that it is essential that all caregivers understand the milestones that young children will achieve and how quickly they will acquire these skills:

Zero to three months
- distinguish between tastes
- notice differences in volume and pitch
- show different facial expressions to respond to caregivers and the environment

- begin to see all colors
- view objects clearly within twelve to thirteen inches
- visually track moving objects
- learn and anticipate responses (begins sucking when the bottle is in sight)

Three to six months
- imitate facial expressions
- respond to the caregiver's facial expressions
- recognize familiar faces
- recognize and react to familiar sounds

Six to nine months
- differentiate between living things and inanimate objects
- determine how far away something is based on the relative size
- distinguish between pictures with different numbers of objects

Nine to twelve months
- imitate basic actions and gestures
- respond with sounds and gestures
- understand that an object still exists even if it is not visible (object permanence)
- look at picture books with interest
- begin to explore and manipulate objects in new ways (e.g., bending, turning, stacking)

One to two years
- understand and respond to words
- imitate the language and actions of adults
- identify objects that are the same
- identify familiar people and objects in picture books
- learn the difference between the words "me" and "you"
- learn by exploring their environment

Two to three years
- language significantly increases
- match objects to their uses
- name the objects in a picture book
- respond to any simple directions (e.g., "Come here" or "Wave goodbye")
- call themselves by name when looking in the mirror at their reflection
- imitate adult actions that are more complex (e.g., talking on the phone or drinking coffee)
- stack rings in order starting with the largest and ending with the smallest
- sort objects by category (such as shape, color, plants, animals)

Each of these milestones shows how quickly the brain is growing and soaking in new information. Within three years, the child goes from only recognizing concrete objects that are within reach to beginning basic pretend play skills like imitation and basic math skills like sorting same and different objects. The caregiver and the family need to recognize these milestones in order to support the child and help her move toward the next skill.

ACTIVITIES TO SUPPORT COGNITIVE DEVELOPMENT

With a new infant (between birth and three months), the caregiver's primary purpose is to establish an attached relationship and respond to the baby's basic needs; however, many cognitive skills are addressed during responsive caregiving. Talking and singing to the infant helps the infant to be more aware of familiar voices and to discriminate between tone and volume in the voice. Reading to the infant allows the baby to look at colorful pictures, hear new vocabulary, and listen to the caregiver labeling the pictures. Hanging a mobile over the crib or changing table gives the infant an opportunity to see colors and focus on moving objects. Letting the infant look at her own face in the mirror gives her the chance to study her facial expressions and movements. Also, it is important to provide toys that make different sounds to hear pitch and repetitive sounds.

At three to six months of age, the caregiver should continue to talk to the infant and maintain eye contact whenever possible. The caregiver can use self-talk to tell the baby about his day or use parallel talk to describe what the infant is doing. While the baby is lying on the floor for short amounts of tummy time, the caregiver can place a mirror in front of her so that she can study her facial expressions. The caregiver can introduce the baby to new textures by providing a variety of rattles and teething toys that feel smooth, bumpy, and cold (from being in the refrigerator). This allows the infant to explore the rattle visually, shake it, and also explore it with her mouth. It is important for the caregiver to call the other caregivers and children by name so the infant can begin to associate them with their true name. Of course, it is still essential for the caregiver to continue reading to the infant.

At six to nine months, the infant is sitting up and may become mobile. Once the infant can crawl, she can explore the entire classroom. It is important for the caregiver to introduce materials and toys that make new sounds, have a variety of textures, and show many different colors. It is also important that the infant experiences different smells and tastes. Since most caregivers introduce pureed foods around six or seven months, the baby will begin to distinguish between and experience new and desirable tastes.

The classroom should be set up for the infant to move and explore. Toys should be on low shelves that allow children to grasp and pull the ones they choose. The caregiver can also play hide and seek games or peek-a-boo with the infant to help establish object permanence. The adult should continue to introduce new books and label the pictures on the pages.

By the time the infant is nine to twelve months old, his grasp should be developed enough for the caregiver to introduce large knobbed puzzles. Even if the child cannot yet put the pieces in place, this allows him to begin exploring the shape of the pieces. This is also a great time for the caregiver to introduce nesting toys that stack inside each other. The infant can begin to distinguish large items from small items and follow a sequence.

The infant can also begin to play with toys that move. This allows the child to start observing toys that move up and down, side to side, and left to right. The caregiver should play games with the infant where the baby must identify parts of the body (e.g., tummy, hands, feet, toes). The adults should continue to play hide and seek games and continue to read to the infant each day.

A one-year-old child is beginning to talk and move independently around the room. Once the child can walk and has more control over his body, he really has the opportunity to explore all parts of the classroom. The caregiver can now give the child simple directions like "Come see me." The toddler may not initially respond to verbal instructions, but he will begin to respond when the caregiver uses gestures and eye contact as encouragement also. The classroom should play music and encourage young toddlers to dance and move to the beat of the music. It is important for caregivers to engage in more and more conversations as the children begin to learn new vocabulary. Caregivers can introduce shapes and colors, identify familiar characters and objects in books, and identify family members in pictures. This is also a great time to introduce simple classroom rules like "feet on the floor" and "gentle hands."

Older toddlers will move more independently and be able to use more words in the classroom. Caregivers can count with the children, show the children bright colors in their natural environment, and begin introducing the environment. Colors, numbers, and shapes can come up in casual conversations. When the toddler is pushing a car around the rug, the caregiver might say, "That red car is going so fast."

Older toddlers are capable of making simple choices, so it is important for the caregiver to offer two possible options for children to choose between. "Do you want to play with the blue truck or the teddy bear?" Since music is a great way for children to acquire new vocabulary, the caregivers should be singing with the children each day and repeating favorite songs again and again. It is also important to read favorite books over and over again. Toddlers enjoy repetition.

PRELITERACY SKILLS

Although children may not learn to read until around the age of five, there are many preliteracy steps that children begin learning in the infant and toddler classrooms. Emergent literacy is what children learn about reading before they ever learn to read (Parlakian, 2003). First, young children need to learn how to handle books. This means they learn how to hold the book right side up, turn the pages, and go from the left page to the right page. It also means that children learn not to use the book inappropriately, like chewing on the book or ripping the pages. Children learn how to handle books by watching their caregivers read to them again and again and by getting the opportunity to handle books themselves.

Second, children need to learn how to look at the pages in the book and observe what is happening in the pictures (Parlakian, 2003). Caregivers can help children learn this skill by labeling the objects in the book when they first begin to read books to children. Once children are exploring books on their own, it is important for the caregivers to ask questions about what the child sees on the page and ask the child to identify the characters and the objects.

Third, children need picture and story comprehension before they can learn to read (Parlakian, 2003). Caregivers can begin teaching this skill by posting pictures around the room of classroom families or of children and families from around the world. Caregivers can prompt the children and ask them what is happening in the pictures. When a toddler sits in a caregiver's lap to read a story, it is important for the caregiver to ask the child about what is happening on each page. It is also helpful for the caregiver to summarize what is happening in the story as she reads the book to the child.

Finally, children need to learn story-reading behavior before they learn to read (Parlakian, 2003). Children need to understand the verbal interactions that occur when using a book. This may mean that the child babbles while pointing to the pictures and the words on the page. Children also need to understand that the print in the books has meaning and that the caregiver is decoding the print when she reads the story. Caregivers can help young children understand this concept when they point to the words in the book as they read them. These four emergent reading skills will assist older preschoolers and kindergarten students learn to read successfully.

Many early childhood educators will tell you that the secret to learning to read is to give young children plenty of opportunities to talk, sing, read, write, and play. The more words that young children learn, the easier it will be when that child learns to read. If a child has already heard a word before reading it for the first time, then they are more likely to be able to sound it out. That means that young children need to experience a lot of conversations and develop their vocabulary for future reading success. Singing is useful for increasing vocabulary, but it also helps children learn the rhythm and flow of words. Children learn how to pronounce and articulate to a pattern during a song. Later, children will learn to read using patterns also.

When caregivers read to young children, it has many benefits. Children develop a love of listening to stories and learning new information so they are more motivated to learn to read. Children begin to memorize familiar words when they see a caregiver read them over and over again. Also, hearing print and oral stories allows children to listen and analyze the story to improve comprehension. Although reading to a child again and again shows significant benefits, the same benefits do not occur by using literacy flashcards with children at young ages. This skill is not developmentally appropriate for toddlers and young preschoolers, and this type of drill and practice activity can have a negative effect on children's curiosity (Parlakian, 2003).

Along with offering children opportunities to read, it is also important to offer them opportunities to write. This does not mean the caregivers should offer young children worksheets to practice writing letters. Instead, caregivers need to make sure the toddlers always have access to crayons and paper. Toddlers need the opportunity to learn to hold crayons, to scribble, to create simple pictures, and to imitate adult handwriting. This activity should always be available to the children, but not forced.

PRE-MATHEMATICS SKILLS

School readiness in mathematics involves children that can rote count (count in sequence), count objects with one-to-one correspondence, and visually recognize numbers. Pre-mathematics skills start with simple tasks introduced in the infant and toddler classrooms. Before children learn to count, they need to learn to play matching games, sort and classify, measure, create patterns, seriate, and learn shapes and spatial relationships. Sorting allows children to learn the concept of same and different. When children sort toys and objects in the classroom, they look at characteristics like color, shape, texture, size, and the object's purpose. This begins the process of observation and analysis.

When children begin to identify shapes, they must recognize and name the shape, as well as compare and contrast it to other shapes. Learning about spatial relationships allows children to understand the physical relationship of one object to another. Children building in the block area must be able to show spatial awareness and determine how long a block needs to be to build a bridge between two towers. Young children assembling puzzles must be able to identify the shape of the puzzle piece and determine that it is the same shape as the opening in the puzzle board. These are the basic versions of direction and positioning skills used in more advanced engineering tools.

Measurement allows children to determine qualities like size, weight, quantity, volume, and time. Children may begin measuring without tools, but older toddlers may learn to use simple tools like rulers or scales. Toddlers learn to compare the big ball with the small ball and the heavy blocks with the light blocks. They frequently learn to measure by playing in the sand and water tables. By scooping and dumping sand and water, children learn concepts like volume and weight.

Patterns are all over the early childhood classroom. Children learn about patterns by repetitions of colors, sounds, lines, and textures. Infants and toddlers first learn about patterns by being in an environment with a predictable routine. This is the first pattern that helps young children understand their world. Many hide and seek games (like peek-a-boo) create safe patterns for young children where the children know what happens at the end of the story. Infants begin to experiment with patterns when they play games with adults like the baby dropping the rattle and waiting for the adult to pick the rattle up off the floor.

Once children experience many of the pre-mathematics concepts, then the caregiver begins to introduce numeracy also. Just like alphabet letters, the children need the opportunity to explore with numbers as well. Children should see printed numbers around the classroom and in picture books. Caregivers need to count objects in the classroom with the children, and they need to sing songs and chant nursery rhymes with numbers. Caregivers can also use numbers in classroom transitions, like asking each toddler to pick up two blocks and place them back on the block shelf.

The classroom should include pre-mathematical skills and numeracy for infants and toddlers. Here are several math activities to incorporate in the infant and toddler classroom:

- *Peek-a-boo:* This is played when the caregiver covers her face with her hands and then removes her hands again to show a smile. This is a great skill to create patterns and to teach object permanence. Object permanence activities help children to notice same and different skills also.
- *Building towers:* This is an activity that all children love, especially when they get to knock the tower down. Building the tower helps develop spatial relationships and learn mathematical concepts like size and shape.
- *Stacking rings:* The stacking rings are a classic children's toy. They allow the children to develop seriation skills by ordering the rings from largest to smallest.

- *Playing in tunnels:* Children can crawl through the collapsible tunnel on the floor and hide from their peers. This game also allows children to learn spatial relationships, depth perception, and directionality.
- *Pat-a-cake:* This hand-clapping game creates patterns between individual clapping and two-hand clapping. The toddler learns to follow a sequence to participate in the game.
- *Music and rhythm:* Music includes many mathematical concepts. Tapping to the beat of a song creates a pattern and helps children use observation skills to compare concepts like fast and slow or short and long.

Chapter Eight

Assessment and Early Intervention

In elementary school, assessments (or tests) have very specific purposes. The assessment is used to see what students have learned after a unit of curriculum is taught. They are used to hold teachers accountable for the material that they are supposed to teach the children during each year of school. Assessments are also used to see which students are not learning the content that the teachers are teaching during class time each day. Of course, assessments are linked to grades, and so students put pressure on themselves to do well on assessments so that they do not receive a poor grade. Many students find the assessment process very stressful. Even if they do not understand the curriculum, they put pressure on themselves to do well on the assessments so that they will receive the expected grade.

The early childhood assessment process is extremely different. When a caregiver assesses a child, he or she is assessing a developmental skill, not a particular piece of knowledge. There are not grades attached to early childhood assessment, and in general, children are not rewarded or acknowledged for their performance on an assessment. The assessment is used to tell the caregiver deeper information about the children.

DEFINING DEVELOPMENTAL ASSESSMENTS

A developmental assessment is a tool used to help the caregiver understand the children's strengths, weaknesses, and interests. In her book *The Early Intervention Guidebook for Families and Professionals* (2016), Bonnie Keilty states that assessment allows the caregiver to determine four major ideas:

- what the child knows how to do;
- how well the child knows how to do it;

- how the child learns; and
- how well intervention strategies are working.

The assessment process may involve the caregiver observing the child and taking notes, using a developmental checklist, using a formal assessment tool to take an in-depth look at the child's developmental skills, and/or talking with the family about the child's development. When the caregiver includes the family in the assessment process, then she is also able to determine what the family's goals are for the child, any concerns that the family may have about the child's development, and any skills that the family may want to promote. For example, in the United States, families typically value independence a great deal. This means that the family may find it very important for the child to be able to eat or use the toilet independently. In other cultures, the family may not be as concerned about independence, but they may want to promote other crucial skills.

THE IMPORTANCE OF ASSESSMENT

Families and caregivers need to remember that early childhood assessment is important for every child in the classroom, not only those that may be struggling with meeting developmental milestones. High-quality assessments can improve the learning environment for all young children by improving relationships and curriculum in the classroom setting. At the same time, assessment can identify children with special needs at a young age so that those children can get the support they need to make gains in each developmental area.

- *Assessment should be used as a method for the caregiver to learn specific details about each child in the classroom.* Although the caregiver learns individual details about the children in the classroom each day while sitting on the floor and interacting with them, a developmental assessment will help the caregiver to take a detailed look at each child. If nothing else, the time the caregiver spends observing the child and completing the assessment with the child allows for one-on-one time that may not occur during a regular day in the classroom.
- *Assessment should be used as a tool for curriculum planning.* Once the caregiver uses the assessment tool to understand the strengths and weaknesses of each child in the classroom, then she should use that information to create learning activities that will help each child meet his or her next developmental achievement. The assessment information should also

determine which children will need some type of accommodation to participate in the learning activity successfully.
- *Assessment is a tool the caregiver can use to design the classroom environment.* Once the caregiver reviews the assessments for the children in the classroom, it can offer a more concrete picture of what the classroom should look like. If a classroom of infants is becoming more mobile, then the caregiver may arrange the classroom furniture to allow for more walking and place more push and pull toys out in the environment to encourage the development of motor skills.
- *Assessment is a tool to create a consistent classroom schedule.* As children mature from young infants to young toddlers, they become more routine-oriented. When the assessment results show that children in the classroom are becoming more mobile and demonstrating more independence skills, then it is time for the caregiver to consider using routines more appropriate for young toddlers. This may mean that most children are ready to sleep on cots instead of in cribs. This could also mean that the children are independent and social enough to sit at the table for a group mealtime instead of participating in individual feedings.
- *Assessment offers caregivers a way to include the family in classroom participation and curriculum planning.* When the caregiver asks the family important information about the child's development, then the family members are acknowledged as the experts about their child. This helps strengthen the communication between the caregiver and the family and the mutual respect between the caregiver and the family members. The family has information that the caregiver needs in order to get a picture of the child's full development, and when the family and caregivers share information about the child, it helps them to align their caregiving strategies.
- *Assessment is a method to detect developmental delays at a young age.* When a child scores below average in one or more areas of development on a classroom assessment, it is an indication to the caregiver to watch that area of growth more closely. If the child continues to struggle, then it may be time to speak with the family about a referral for further evaluation by a medical professional or therapists. A referral does not mean that the child has some type of special need; however, it does mean that there is even cause to look more closely at that area of development with a specialist.

USING ASSESSMENT CORRECTLY

In order for assessment to be an effective classroom tool, caregivers must be trained on using the type of assessment the program has in place. When an assessment tool is not used correctly, it can provide inaccurate data. Most early childhood assessments are not complicated, but the caregiver still needs to attend a training on the tool and practice with the tool before using it in the classroom setting. It is also important for the caregiver and the family to remember that the assessment is only one picture of the child's skills. The child may behave differently at home in the natural environment than when she first begins in a classroom setting. This is why it is essential for the caregiver and the family to communicate during the assessment process. Here are several additional reminders to establish quality assessment information:

- Assessments should be age-appropriate, both for the skills they are observing and for the method using which information is collected (e.g., asking a young toddler to perform a skill on command may not be effective).
- Assessments should be conducted in the child's primary language.
- Assessments should have one specific purpose and be used for that purpose. If the tool is simply a screening tool to see if further evaluation is needed, then that assessment should not be used to diagnose a developmental delay.
- Assessments should be completed in the child's natural environment with a familiar caregiver in order for the child to feel most comfortable.
- Assessments should include the child's family, not only to offer essential information during the evaluation process but also as the recipients of the completed evaluation information.
- Assessment should be done at multiple times during the course of the school year in order to track a child's progress and allow the caregiver to use the updated information for curriculum planning and classroom design.

FITTING ASSESSMENT INTO THE INFANT-TODDLER CLASSROOM

Because so many basic needs (e.g., feeding, diapering, and napping) are addressed in the infant and toddler classrooms, there may not be a great deal of time in a typical classroom schedule for assessment. This means that caregivers must be intentional when they plan how to assess young children. First, the caregiver needs to determine what time of year the assessments will take place. Many early childhood programs do some type of assessment at the beginning of the year to get baseline (or beginning) data, and then they may add one or two more assessment periods throughout the school year to show growth.

It is important for the caregiver to set realistic expectations for how long it will take to assess each child. For example, if the initial assessments must be done in the first forty-five days of school, then the caregiver should anticipate that the first two weeks will be completely dedicated to establishing classroom routines. After those two weeks are over, the caregiver needs to review the assessment tool and become familiar with what skills need to be assessed. The caregiver should plan on using two to three weeks to collect all of the assessment information, because there may be days that the needs of the children do not allow for assessment.

It is also important for the caregiver to consider which routine activities will allow her to collect the most information. For example, mealtime is an excellent time to observe young toddlers. The caregiver will not only be able to assess the toddlers' feeding skills, but she will also see the toddlers in a social setting and be able to watch their abilities to follow instructions and routines. However, toddlers are sitting still for most of meal time, so the caregiver may need to wait until the children go to the playground to assess their gross motor skills.

If there is more than one caregiver in the classroom, it is important to decide which caregiver will assess each child. If the classroom is designed with a primary caregiver that is responsible for a small group of children, then the primary caregiver should be the adult to assess those children. If there is not a primary caregiver design, then the caregivers should collaborate to decide which child is most comfortable with which caregiver. Some childcare programs may only send a portion of their staff to assessment training, and they assume that a few staff members will do the assessments for each of the children in the entire program. This is not the best way to get an accurate picture of each child's development. Children are always going to show their true abilities in the most natural setting with the adults who help them feel safe and comfortable.

ASSESSMENT AND SCHOOL READINESS

Since early childhood assessment does not resemble elementary education assessment, it is easy to ask how this type of assessment prepares children to be successful in kindergarten. The key to early childhood assessment is that the caregiver constantly evaluates each child's developmental level and then uses that information to create the most appropriate curriculum. This means that a child's development should always be moving forward, instead of sitting in a stagnant environment where new challenges are never presented to the child. Early childhood assessment is also an important tool because it identifies children that are falling below the developmental standards for their age and helps the caregivers or specialized therapists offer the child additional supports to catch up to his or her same-aged peers.

WHAT IS A "RED FLAG"?

A "red flag" is a term used in education to say that something does not seem right. In early childhood assessment a "red flag" would be that a child is not meeting some of his developmental goals or that he is at risk of not meeting those goals. Initially, this may mean that the caregiver just observes the child more closely in those areas to see if he is making improvements.

A "red flag" may be discovered during an assessment or it may be discovered as the caregiver observes the child in the classroom each day. Most developmental skills, like walking, have a window of time that is normal for the child to achieve the skill. Although the average timeline for walking is around twelve months, it is still considered to be in the developmental window if the child begins walking anywhere from ten to sixteen months of age.

As the caregiver watches during this developmental window, it is essential to stay in communication with the family. If the family is upset that the child is thirteen months old and still not walking, it is important to remind the family that each child develops at her own pace and that she still has several months to walk during the typically developing timeframe. Once this window passes, then it may be time to seek additional input from a doctor or therapist.

If both the family and the caregiver are in agreement that there is a concern, then it is simple to proceed with a developmental referral. However, if the caregiver continues to express concerns and the family does not feel the same, the caregiver cannot proceed without the support of the family. The caregiver can continue to show the family how the child is falling behind on developmental assessments and encourage the family to observe the child in the classroom to see that she is not progressing at the same rate as her peers.

Each family has a different perspective about how to deal with a child's development. Some families may want to offer their children additional support as soon as a potential delay is identified. Some families may believe that the children are just developing at their own pace, and they will eventually catch up. Other families may experience feelings of grief or loss at the mere thought of their child having a potential disability. Early childhood caregivers need to support the family in whatever manner possible.

Caregivers should not push a family that is not interested in pursuing therapy for a child, but it is also important to continue to share assessment information with the family to keep them updated on the child's development. If the family members do have a concern and want to proceed with a referral, then the next step will be further evaluation by a specialist to see if the child qualifies for early intervention services.

WHAT IS EARLY INTERVENTION?

Early intervention services are designed for children from the age of birth until the age they enter kindergarten. It is offered to children in this age range who need additional support in one or more of the developmental domains: cognitive, motor, language, or social/emotional skills. Early intervention is typically provided by a specialist like a physical therapist, occupational therapist, speech pathologist, or a developmental interventionist. A child with a medical condition may also receive support from a physician, a respiratory therapist, or an audiologist depending on what type of diagnosis the child has. Unlike other types of therapy, early intervention typically works with the child and the family to help the family as a whole work through the challenges of the child's delays.

There are many different ways that a child can qualify for early intervention. Once the family has started the referral process, they have many different options. They can have the child assessed through a private therapist or medical professional. Many doctors and therapists accept health insurance, so the health insurance company would establish the standard for what type of score on the assessment would qualify the child for services. If the insurance company did not see a documented need for the early intervention, then the family would still have the option to pay for the services out-of-pocket.

Many states have a statewide early intervention system that includes home visitors for children under the age of three and public school resources for children that qualify for public school preschool. Again, the state program would establish the standard for how a child would qualify for the program. If a child qualifies, then the state program may pay for the therapy resources or it may bill the family's insurance or Medicaid for the early intervention.

Once a child qualifies for early intervention, the family needs to determine how the child will receive the support services. When working with infants and toddlers, many therapists prefer to visit the children in their natural environments, like at home or in their childcare classroom. This allows the child to feel as comfortable as possible. This also helps the therapist observe the child during typical routines to see his strengths and his weaknesses.

WHY IS EARLY INTERVENTION IMPORTANT?

Some families may admit that they are concerned about their children's development, but they may not understand the importance of early intervention. When early intervention is used correctly, it benefits the children and the families.

- Child development principles teach that the child's brain grows more during the first three years of life than it will at any other point in development (Nowakowski, 2006). During the first three years, an immense amount of learning and growing occurs. Children meet most of the motor milestones they will experience throughout their lives during the first three years of life, and this is also the time period when children acquire a large portion of their language skills. If the child does not have the ability to take advantage of this developmental window, then damage could be done. Early identification and treatment of a delay will assist a child with meeting his or her full developmental potential.
- Early intervention also benefits the families of young children with developmental delays. The child with the delay is not the only person affected by the condition. The family works as a unit, so all members of the family will feel an impact when one member of the family is struggling. Parents and other family members may experience grief, anger, fear, depression, confusion, isolation, or helplessness after a child is diagnosed with a delay. The family will experience additional stress due to medical expenses, specialized training, finding quality childcare, the schedule of taking a child to additional therapy, or working with the health insurance company to ensure continued services. The early intervention team can support the family members as they begin the process of figuring out how to care for their child and how to be advocates for their child's care.

BEGINNING THE PROCESS OF EARLY INTERVENTION

After the insurance company or the therapy program has established eligibility, the next step is to create an intervention plan that is individualized to the needs of the child. This means that the child's entire team (the family, the early childhood caregiver, the therapists, and the case manager) will sit down together to establish how to proceed in the best interest of the child. The therapy plan will be based on the delayed areas of development; however, the immediate goals will be created for the child by the family and the community of professionals supporting the child.

It is important that all of the members of the child's team are present during this meeting. When the goals are established, these will be the same goals for the home, the classroom, and the therapists' offices. The caregiver needs to be informed about the intervention goals, but she must also find ways to incorporate these goals into the classroom and to assess if the child is meeting these goals. This may mean that the therapists need to visit the classroom to see the child's behavior in this natural environment and then collaborate with the caregiver to offer the caregiver suggestions on room arrangement, curriculum ideas, or ways to help soothe the child in the classroom environment.

The intervention team must take the time to listen to the family's goals and priorities for the child and place those goals into the intervention plan. If the family places a high priority on taking the child to family gatherings or out to eat at restaurants, then the therapy team would need to look at skills that would help the child adapt to that environment, like learning to sit in a highchair for a meal. Then the therapists and the caregiver would all work with the family to supply parent education materials when the family members have questions.

The intervention team may decide that the toddler classroom is the best place for the child to receive therapy since the child spends most of his waking hours in the classroom each day. The caregiver would need to collaborate with the therapist to provide time in the schedule and classroom space for the therapist to work with the child. Then the caregiver would need to communicate with the family about what took place in the classroom and what new goals the child is working toward. Each member of the intervention team is essential, and the early childhood caregiver must play an active role in the child's development when an intervention plan is created.

While the intervention plan is in place, the caregiver may be the person that is able to assess the child most frequently. It is important for the caregiver to document when a child achieves a goal or when new concerns surface. It is the caregiver's responsibility to share this information with the rest of the intervention team to make sure that the intervention plan remains up to date and addresses the needs of the child.

EARLY INTERVENTION AND SCHOOL READINESS

If a child shows signs of developmental delays, early intervention is a huge part of establishing school readiness. When it is obvious that the child may not be able to enter kindergarten meeting the normal developmental milestones, then it is essential to help the child be as prepared as possible for the new challenges in elementary school. Early intervention specifically focuses on areas that are challenging the child and then provides trained specialists to assist the child with growth in those areas. Early intervention also provides parent education to allow the family to understand the developmental goals for the child and to train the family on how to work on these goals at home as well as in the classroom environment. If a child is struggling in one of the developmental domains, early intervention is the best step toward school readiness.

Chapter Nine

Parent Involvement in the Infant-Toddler Classrooms

The primary goal of school readiness is to prepare each child to be successful in school, starting in kindergarten. It is also essential to prepare the family to have a successful experience in school, and that experience begins by involving the family in a child's education. Research has proven that increased parent participation is linked to school success for young children (Epstein, 1994).

Parent involvement will look different for each family, but it includes volunteering at school, helping children with their homework, attending family events at school or in the classroom, attending parent–teacher conferences, taking leadership roles in the school's parent–teacher organization or school council, or visiting the school to guest lecture or read to the class (Larocque, Kleiman, and Darling, 2011). Parent involvement also includes communication between the child's teacher and the family.

These activities may seem like very reasonable activities by which parents can participate and be active in their children's education; however, the typical family member may have many barriers preventing him or her from being an active participant in the children's education. A parent may not be able to attend a school function due to conflicts with his or her job or a lack of transportation. Many families may have a language barrier between their primary language and the language the school uses to communicate in newsletters and parent meetings. These families may not even know about opportunities offered at the school.

Still other parents may have had negative school experiences as children and feel intimidated when they attend any school. Some parents may not be able to attend afterschool parent meetings. A lack of childcare can be a huge deterrent for many families who want to participate in parent events. Teachers and administrators must consider all of these barriers when they plan family events and find ways to help each family attend.

Children benefit from family involvement in school, but research has also shown that there are benefits for families that are involved in their children's education (Pena, 2001). Family members that communicate with the teachers and the school learn more about their children's individual needs. Also, these family members learn more about the teacher's plan for their children's education. They begin to develop better attitudes toward teachers and schools in general. Some parents may even decide to continue their own education after seeing how the education system benefits their children.

Teachers benefit from family involvement in the classroom as well. When parents participate with teachers, they can be a source of great knowledge for the teachers. Parents know their children better than anyone else, so they can tell the teachers essential information about their children. Parents know what motivates their children, what scares them, and how to calm them down when they are upset. They can tell teachers how they deal with challenging behaviors and what type of expectations the family has outside of school. All of this information helps the teacher relate to the children and plan for each child's needs. This type of two-way communication allows the family members and the teachers to work as a team.

Beginning in elementary school, parent involvement will include assisting a child with homework, reviewing report cards, and an increased focus on academic skills (Arnold et al., 2008), but parent involvement in an early childhood education program will look slightly different. Beginning in the infant and toddler classrooms, the childcare program will encourage parent involvement by developing relationships between the parents and the caregivers, establishing daily communication methods, encouraging parents to be involved in the classroom, and offering the caregivers as a resource to each family.

Early childhood programs will also encourage families to express their gratitude and their concerns with their children's caregivers when needed. Many early childhood settings will start utilizing parents as a resource by encouraging them to volunteer on parent advisory boards and offer skills like fundraising or community relationships to help improve the program. No matter what the age of the children, parents can find a way to participate in their children's education.

DEVELOPING PARENT–TEACHER RELATIONSHIPS

When parents walk into an early childhood classroom for the first time, they are bringing the most precious things in their lives, their children, and leaving them with caregivers that they do not know. This is an incredible challenge for anyone. Initially, all parents are uncomfortable with this leap of faith, and it is the caregiver's responsibility to put those parents at ease and develop a relationship of trust.

When we look back at basic child development theories, Erikson (1950) teaches us that a child cannot develop advanced skills (e.g., independence, identity) until he is able to trust his primary caregiver. The baby needs to know that when he cries, someone will hold him. He needs to know that when he is hungry, someone will feed him. He must know that when he is scared, someone will be there to keep him safe. The parents of infants and toddlers are very similar to these young children. They must know that their infant is safe when they leave him. They must know that someone will hold him and make him feel safe when he is scared. They must know that he is being fed and that his diaper is being changed before they can go to work with confidence.

The caregiver must be likeable. The family needs to feel comfortable around the caregiver and know that this is a person with whom the infant will enjoy spending his day. The caregiver also needs to be available to talk with the parents when they have questions. Many parents may not have questions initially. They are too overwhelmed. The caregiver needs to offer the family members a method of communication that they can use when they do have questions. It is essential for caregivers to follow through with the promises they make to parents at this fragile stage. If the parents ask the caregivers to make sure that their baby has her favorite pacifier every day at naptime, then the caregiver needs to follow through in order to soothe the child and to gain the trust of the family.

It can also be helpful to the new family members if the caregiver allows them to lead the initial conversations instead of giving them instructions each day. The members of a new family may need the opportunity to share their emotions with someone. They may not need advice. They may not need someone to tell them that their child is in a fabulous childcare program. They may simply need someone to listen. If the caregiver can listen to their fears and their stress, it may be the bond that solidifies that family's trust.

At the same time, some families may need to know that the caregiver has had a similar experience. A caregiver's personal experiences can help a nervous family relate. It is essential that the caregiver is cautious not to dominate the conversation, but these shared memories can make the caregiver seem more relatable to the family. At least the parents can acknowledge that the caregiver understands how they feel.

Parents are also comforted when the caregiver makes an effort to learn about their individual family. It is important that each caregiver learns the names of the important adults in the children's lives. It is even better if the caregiver knows a few details about what the family members do outside of school. It can be very valuable to learn details like the parents' jobs and how the family members spend their free time.

Likewise, parents want to know that the caregiver knows the intricacies of the child's personality. The caregiver should know what makes a toddler laugh, the best way to hold the baby to calm him down, and what is the baby's favorite toy at school. When a caregiver shares these types of details with the family, it reassures them that he or she is paying special attention to their child. Infant and toddler caregivers need to make each family feel that their child is extremely special and important. If the family members feel like the caregiver adores their child in the same way that the family does, then the parents will feel comfortable leaving their child.

Another component of a trusting relationship is confidentiality. It is imperative that early childhood professionals keep personal information about a child confidential. Of course, there are laws that require this confidentiality like the Federal Education Rights and Privacy Act (FERPA), but this is also essential to earn the respect of each family. Some parents are not concerned if others know details about their children's development; however, this information is their story to share with others, not the caregiver's.

Other parents are much more private and prefer that only essential staff and family members know the details related to their children's development. These families may have children with or without special needs, and it is important to honor their wishes. Caregivers need to make an effort to speak with these families about their children in a more private setting instead of during drop-off and pick-up times.

It is also important that the caregiver does not share information when family members ask a question about a child that is not in their family. This sounds like a simple concept, but parents will often ask questions about the development of the other children in the classroom in order to see how their own children are developing. For example, if Johnny's mother comes to pick him up one day, she may ask, "Are other children in the classroom crawling yet? Is Henry already crawling?" Instead of giving her personal information about one child, the caregiver should respond by saying, "Several of the children in the classroom are very close to crawling." The parents in a childcare classroom are not usually trying to pry confidential information from the caregiver. In most cases, the parents only want to know if their children are developing at the same rate as others. The exception to this rule is when a young toddler begins to hit, scratch, or bite.

When a toddler shows some aggressive behaviors toward other children in the classroom, it is essential for the caregiver to do everything possible to protect that child's privacy. Of course the caregiver should let both families know that a child was bitten, but it must be done in a way to protect both children.

Early childhood professionals should never write the name of the other student on an incident report that will be signed by a child's family.

Also, those incident reports should not be displayed in a visible area of the classroom while the provider is waiting for the parents to arrive and sign-off on the form. Since parents are natural advocates for their children, it is their nature to protect their children. Caregivers should expect nothing less. However, the caregiver does not want the family to develop a grudge against another child for a behavior that is developmentally normal.

The ultimate goal of confidentiality is for the family to feel safe leaving their children and their children's personal information in the hands of the caregivers and the school program at large. When the family does feel safe, they are more apt to provide additional information to the caregiver about the child's behavior, about the home environment, and about the family's priorities for raising the child. This is the type of necessary information that will assist the caregiver in the classroom, so providing confidentiality will benefit both the family and the caregivers.

Finally, to ensure a trusting relationship between the family and the caregiver, the caregiver needs to acknowledge the family members as experts about their children and use the family as a resource. Although a caregiver may spend eight hours a day with a child for six months to a year, the family members are with that child forever. They see the child in many different settings. They are completely invested in the child's happiness so they know what soothes their child, what her favorite toy is, and what foods she refuses to eat.

When a young child is in an early childhood environment with other children, his behavior may be very different than when he is at home with the family's full attention or sharing that attention with only one or two siblings. Since the caregiver will never see the child in that environment, it is important to seek that information from the parents. When parents are acknowledged as the experts about their children, they are much more likely to share details and interesting stories about their children.

ESTABLISHING THE TEACHER AS A RESOURCE

When a family selects a childcare program, they look at many different characteristics. Along with the health and safety of the program and the nurturing relationship provided by the caregiver, parents frequently select caregivers with knowledge and experience in the field of early childhood education (Degotardi, 2010). When an early childhood professional is experienced at working with young children and has specific training in child development, parents feel comfortable that the caregiver can handle the classroom setting and is an expert in the field. Experience and education are essentials for being an expert. The caregiver must also demonstrate behavior that allows the parents to seek advice when they need it. This will set the family up for a pattern of contacting the caregiver with questions and concerns in the future.

Parents are more likely to view a caregiver as a professional when they see the caregiver demonstrating professional behavior. This begins with simple behaviors like dressing professionally for work and arriving on time each day. It may also include the caregiver using her cell phone responsibly while at work and refraining from gossiping about other coworkers and families. These types of behaviors would not be tolerated in other professions like banking or a law office, and the field of early childhood education should not tolerate these behaviors either. One professional behavior that is essential when caring for young children is for the caregiver to be present at work each day unless an emergency prevents attendance. Families will have a difficult time respecting and growing close to a caregiver with irregular attendance.

All early childhood professionals must continue their education. For some caregivers this may mean pursuing professional degrees like a Child Development Associates degree or a college degree in early childhood education. For other caregivers this may mean continuing to plan new professional development training each year to increase their knowledge in the field of early education. All states have childcare regulations that require professional development, but caregivers with a desire to continue learning need to be very deliberate in what trainings they attend.

If caregivers are teaching young children about the joy and importance of learning, then it is essential to set the example of being a lifelong learner. When parents realize that their children's caregivers are continuing to learn about new curriculum and ways to help children learn, they are much more likely to bring their questions and concerns to the caregiver. Most parents would rather consult with an expert face to face than blindly search the Internet for information that may or may not be applicable to their children. Once a parent has established a pattern of seeking information from the caregiver, then he or she will continue to see the child's teachers as a resource for years to come.

Early childhood professionals also need to be proactive to discover areas in which all families need further education. Once the program determines these areas of need, it is important for early education programs to provide parent education meetings that provide parents with factual information. Many parents also desire a forum to ask questions and further understand these concepts.

Family members will have opportunities to attend parent education meetings for the rest of their children's education career. If they have positive experiences with these types of meetings when their children are young, then they are more likely to attend again in the future. Instead of focusing on test scores and complicated academic goals like in elementary school, early childhood parent meetings should focus on topics like helping young children prepare for school, explaining a play-based early childhood curriculum, and the importance of social interactions in the early childhood classroom. These meetings are also great opportunities to bring in guest speakers that are experts in one particular area. These experts can reiterate the information that the program has already been providing for the families to show validity.

Families have so many options to find information on early childhood education now, but not all of these options are based on research or quality developmental theories. When parents value the opinion of the child's caregivers and program director, it is possible to make sure that the early childhood professionals are providing them with appropriate information about their children's abilities and about early childhood education expectations. Caregivers must demonstrate their professionalism, knowledge, and experience in the field of early education so that each family feels safe coming to them with questions about their children.

RECOGNIZING THE FAMILY AS EXPERTS

Just as it is important for the family to recognize the caregiver as an early childhood specialist, it is essential for the caregiver to recognize families as experts about their children. A caregiver may take care of a child for one year, or in a multiage classroom, the caregiver may even take care of the child for up to three years. This is still a very small amount of time compared to the family. The family knows how to calm the child and what motivates the child, the child's medical history, as well as their likes and dislikes. The family members are the first caregivers, so it is very important to acknowledge their dedication and knowledge.

It is also important for the caregiver to remember that the family is the expert about the child's culture. The family's culture can be described as their established beliefs and priorities. These cultural beliefs can be based on religion, ethnicity, family roles, and core beliefs. Although the caregiver and the childcare program establish the priorities for the classroom, the family establishes the priorities for their home. It is very important for the caregiver to stay in communication with the family to understand the cultural beliefs in the home. It is also important for the caregiver to respect the family's cultural beliefs, even when those beliefs are different than those of the caregiver.

COMMUNICATION METHODS

In order to ensure school success for young children, it is essential for parents and caregivers to communicate. In years past, the caregivers may have initiated this communication with a weekly classroom newsletter and annual parent–teacher conferences; however, there are many different options available for caregivers and families to share information. Each early childhood program must find the best methods of communication for its families and use those methods to make sure that both caregivers and families understand what is going on in the lives of the children. Some of the possible options include the following:

- *Daily conversations:* Early childhood educators have the unique opportunity to speak to a family member each day at drop-off and pick-up. This is not an opportunity for in-depth conversation, but it is a chance for the caregiver to give the family encouraging reminders like "Shelby had a great day today!" or "We are learning Malcolm's routine, and he is feeling more comfortable in the classroom." This is also an opportunity to share essential information like if a child is running out of diapers or if a parent will be bringing the child to school later than usual due to a doctor's appointment.
- *Newsletters and printed communication:* Depending on the families served by the program, they may still enjoy printed communication from the caregiver. This can range from a weekly newsletter explaining the classroom theme and planned activities for the week or a handwritten note from the teacher telling anecdotes about the child's day. The downside of printed communication is that it often does not make it home for the family to read. It can be forgotten in the classroom or left on the floor of the family minivan. However, some families still prefer to post this type of information on the refrigerator and refer to it throughout the week. If the family speaks a different language in the home, they may prefer printed communication so that they can reference and translate words they do not understand.
- *Email:* Email has become the preferred method of communication for many early childhood education programs. Families are more likely to read an email when it arrives than save a printed newsletter. They are also more likely to respond to an email because they can respond immediately regardless of the time of day or when they will see the teacher next. Caregivers need to be cautious when composing emails. There is not audible tone of voice as in a face-to-face conversation, so families can accidently assume a tone if they do not understand the caregiver's point of view. It is always best to have a coworker proofread an email before sending it to families. It is also important to remember that not all families have daily access to

computers. If email is the sole source of communication, then some families can miss out on important information.
- *Classroom or school-wide blogs:* Many early childhood educators are starting to use weekly or monthly blogs in the same manner they would use a parent education event. Caregivers may use a blog to summarize a week of curriculum or to talk to the parents about important topics like when to keep a sick child home or the importance of handwashing in the infant and toddler classroom. The director of a childcare program may use a school-wide blog to discuss larger concepts on child development or ways that parents can volunteer in the school. For parents who are seeking more information about what their children are doing at school, many enjoy reading regular blog posts. It is important to remember that the longer the blog post, the less likely families are to read it. Blogs should be a page to a page and a half of information with bullet points in order to get the highest amount of parent participation. Again, the school must remember that not every family has daily access to a computer, so the blog should not be the only source of communication.
- *Social media:* Many early childhood programs are using social media pages to communicate with the entire school or with all the families of a particular classroom. Parents can ask questions to the caregivers as well as one another. This type of communication also increases a sense of community. Caregivers need to be cautious about who accesses these social media pages and provide the appropriate confidentiality to the group of families that participate. Also, one of the program caregivers should be responsible for checking to make sure that families are getting their questions answered in a timely manner and that comments on the page remain positive and appropriate.
- *Conferences:* Parent–teacher conferences are still an essential method of communication for all age groups of classrooms. The parents of infants and toddlers will occasionally ask why they would need to have a conference when their children are still so young. There is just as much need for parents and caregivers to share information for an infant as there is for a preschool student or kindergartener. It is important for the caregivers and parents to know what feeding techniques work the best, how the child is sleeping, and what he spends time doing during the day.

It is essential for caregivers to know about the cultural customs of the family and if the family has any priorities for the child to accomplish (e.g., if the family members of a toddler really want to work on toilet-training their child). The caregiver also needs to share the daily schedules and routines with the family. This can help the family with transitions and setting up their schedule at home on days off from school. This is also a time when the parents or the caregivers can bring up concerns about the child, but that is only one purpose for parent–teacher conferences.

When parents begin to engage in communication with the caregivers when their children are very young, they create habits that will instill positive communication throughout their children's education. Establishing that communication in infant and toddler care allows for many years of positive interaction between the family and the child's caregivers.

ESTABLISHING PARENT INVOLVEMENT

Once there is a trusting relationship in place between the family and the caregivers, then the family members can feel comfortable contacting the caregivers with questions. This establishes the foundation for parents to be involved in other areas of their children's education. Parent involvement will look slightly different in the early childhood classroom because the play-based model of learning may allow adults to participate in the classroom more easily than a more structured elementary school setting.

Many early childhood programs begin parent involvement by establishing an open-door policy for each family. This type of policy allows the parents to come in the classroom at any point to view what is going on in the classroom or to participate in activities with their children. Parents may choose to stay for a while in the morning to feed their children or to play with them before going to work.

Some mothers may take advantage of the open-door policy to leave work during the day to come and nurse their infants. Other parents may want to come and observe from outside the classroom door or window just to see what their children enjoy doing at school when the family is not present. Allowing the family to come by the classroom whenever they want creates accountability for the childcare program. Parents feel confident that the program is always using high standards of care if they will allow family members to stop in whenever they choose. This policy also makes families feel invited into the classroom.

Even when families are invited into the classroom during the day, there will be parents who cannot spend time in the classroom due to their jobs. Childcare programs need to find other ways that these family members can participate in the learning environment if they want to do so. These parents may be able to participate by

- donating art materials to the classroom for projects;
- collecting recyclable materials at home for the dramatic play area or art projects;

- helping the teacher to cut out bulletin board materials at home or assisting with homemade classroom materials;
- donating the clothes that young children have outgrown so that the school always has extras on hand;
- participating in parent committees for fundraising or school improvement projects;
- bringing in food items for teacher appreciation meals; and
- attending school-wide parent education programs.

If a parent wants to find a way to volunteer in an early childhood education program, regardless of conflicts with his or her work schedule, the program can find a way to utilize that parent's skills.

HOW TO ADDRESS CONCERNS

At some point in the child's educational career, the family will have concerns about how the child is doing in school or about the child's development. The infant and toddler classroom can help to prepare the family members to handle these concerns and provide the best way to communicate positive and negative information with the child's caregivers.

Again, the most essential part of this communication process is creating a trusting relationship between the family members and the caregivers so that the family feels comfortable coming to the caregivers with concerns as soon as possible. The caregiver needs to establish a professional process for addressing these concerns. Regardless of who presents the initial concerns, the parent or the caregiver, the caregiver needs to follow a structured process to make sure that all concerns are addressed and that the parents feel comfortable with the plan after the initial conversation. Caregivers must make sure to

- set aside a specific time to speak with the family so the caregiver can offer his or her full attention to the family;
- keep the child's and the family's confidentiality and, with parent permission, only share private information with those who need to know;
- speak with the family directly about the concern and avoid talking about the child negatively where he or she can overhear the discussion;
- directly contact the family and try to resolve the situation with them and ask for assistance from the program director if needed;
- create a plan for resolution with which the caregiver and the family can agree; and
- follow up with the family after a few weeks of the new plan to see if the situation is improving the way the family had hoped.

Parents may have concerns about school communication methods, their children's behavior in the classroom, or the ways their children interact with other children. No matter what the concern, the caregivers need to assist the family members with using direct communication with them and following a logical plan to resolve the problem. While trying to resolve the problem, it is essential that the caregivers continuously demonstrate professional behavior so that the family members will feel comfortable communicating their concerns in the future.

Even though parent involvement will look different in early childhood education than in elementary school and secondary education, the foundation for parent involvement is still a relationship between the family members and the teachers. Early childhood professionals have the opportunity to create relationships with families while the children are still very young and encourage the family members to always value communication between the family and the school. This will be an asset for children throughout their educational career.

References

American Academy of Sleep Medicine (May 6, 2009). Bedtime routine improves sleep in infants and toddlers, maternal mood. *Science Daily*. www.sciencedaily.com/releases/2009/05/090501090916.htm

Arnold, D. H., Zeljo, A., Doctoroff, G. L., and Ortiz, C. (2008). Parent involvement in preschool: Predictors and the relation of involvement to preliteracy development. *School Psychology*, 37(1), 74–90.

Bardige, B. S. (2016). *Talk to me, baby: How you can support young children's language development*. Baltimore, MD: Paul H. Brookes.

Berk, L. (2012). *Child development* (9th ed.). London: Pearson.

Bodrova, E., and Leong, D. J. (2007). *Tools of the mind: The Vygotskian approach to early childhood education* (2nd ed.). Columbus, OH: Merrill/Prentice Hall.

Butterfield, P., Martin, C., and Prairie, A. (2003). Emotional connections: Teaching how relationships guide early learning. Washington, DC: Zero to Three.

Cook, J. L., and Cook, G. (2010). *Child development: Principles and perspectives*. Boston, MA: Pearson.

Council on Physical Education for Children (2001). *Recess in elementary schools: A position paper from the National Association for Sport and Physical Education* [Online]. http://www.aahperd.org/naspe/pdf_files/pos_papers/current_res.pdf

Cryer, D. (2003). Defining program quality. In D. Cryer and R. M. Clifford (Eds), *Early childhood education and care in the USA*. Baltimore, MD: Paul H. Brookes, 23–33.

Degotardi, S. (2010). High-quality interactions with infants: Relationships with early-childhood practitioners' interpretations and qualification levels in play and routine contexts. *International Journal of Early Years Education*, 18(1), 27–41.

Ebbeck, M., and Yim, H. Y. B. (2009). Rethinking attachment: Fostering positive relationships between infants, toddlers, and their primary caregivers. *Early Child Development and Care*, 179(7), 899–909.

Epstein, J. L. (1994). Theory to practice: Schools and family partnerships lead to school improvement and student success. In C. L. Fagnano and B. Z. Werber

(Eds), *School, family, and community interaction: A view from the firing lines* (pp. 39–52). Boulder, CO: Westview.

Erikson, Erik H. (1950). *Childhood and society*. New York: W. W. Norton.

Florez, I. R. (2011). Developing young children's self-regulation through everyday experiences. *Young Children*, 66(4), 46–51.

Gilkerson, J., and Richards, J. A. (2009). *The power of talk: Impact of adult talk, conversational turns, and TV during the critical 0–4 years of child development*. Cambridge, MA: Harvard University Press.

Gillespie, L., and Petersen, S. (2012). Rituals and routines: Supporting infants and toddlers and their families. *Young Children*, 67(4), 76–7.

Ginsburg, K. R. (2007). The importance of play in promoting healthy child development and maintaining strong parent-child bonds. *American Academy of Pediatrics*, 119(1). Retrieved September 17, 2007, from www.pediatrics.org

Gonzalez-Mena, J. (2014). *Child, family, and community: Family-centered early care and education*. Boston, MA: Pearson.

Gopnik, A., Meltzoff, A. M., and Kuhl, P. (1999). *The scientist in the crib*. New York: William Morrow.

Greenman, J., Stonehouse, A., and Schweikert, G. (2008). *Prime times: A handbook for excellence in infant and toddler programs* (2nd ed.). St. Paul, MN: Redleaf Press.

Hart, B., and Risley, T. R. (1995). *Meaningful differences in the everyday experience of young American children*. Baltimore, MD: Paul H. Brookes.

High, P. C. (2008). School readiness. *Pediatrics*, 121(4), 1008–15.

Holochwost, S. J., DeMott, K., Buell, M., Yannetta, K., and Amsden, D. (2009). Retention of staff in the early childhood education workforce. *Child and Youth Care Forum*, 38(5), 227–37.

Karp, K. (2002). *The happiest baby on the block*. New York: Bantam Books.

Keilty, B. (2016). *The early intervention guidebook for families and professionals* (2nd ed.). New York: Teachers College Press.

Larocque, M., Kleinman, I., and Darling, S. M. (2011). Parent involvement: The missing link in school achievement. *Preventing School Failure*, 55(3), 115–22.

Lewin-Benham, A. (2010). *Infants and toddlers at work: Using reggio-inspired materials to support brain development*. New York: Teachers College Press.

Maxwell, K. L., and Clifford, R. M. (2004). School readiness assessment. *Young Children*, 59(1), 42–6.

Montessori, M. (1948). *The discovery of the child*. Madras: Kalakshetra.

Moon, R. Y., and AAP Task Force on Sudden Infant Death Syndrome. (2016). SIDS and other sleep-related infant deaths: Evidence base for 2016 updated recommendations for a safe infant sleeping environment. *Pediatrics*, 138(5), e2016–2940.

Morgan, P. L., Farkas, G., Hillemeier, M. M., Hammer, C. S., and Maczuga, S. (2015). 24-month-old children with larger oral vocabularies display greater academic and behavioral functioning at kindergarten entry. *Child Development*, 86(5), 1351–70.

National Association for the Education of Young Children (2008). *Overview of the early childhood program standards*. Retrieved February 2017, from http://www.naeyc.org/files/academy/file/OverviewStandards.pdf

Nowakowski, R. S. (2006). Stable neuron numbers from cradle to grave. *Proceedings of the National Academy of Sciences of the United States of America*, 103(33), 12219–20.

Parlakian, R. (2003). *Before the ABCs: Promoting school readiness in infants and toddlers*. Washington, DC: Zero to Three.

Parten, M. B. (1932). Social participation among preschool children. *Journal of Abnormal and Social Psychology*, 27(3): 243–69.

Pena, D. C. (2001). Parent involvement: Influencing factors and implications. *Journal of Educational Research*, 94, 42–54.

Piaget, J. (1952). *The origin of intelligence in children*. New York: International University Press.

Pruden, S. M., Hirsh-Pasek, K., Golinkoff, R. M., and Hennon, E. A. (2006). The birth of words: Ten-month-olds learn words through personal salience. *Child Development*, 77, 266–80.

Sandall, S. R., and Schwartz, I. S. (2008). *Building blocks for teaching preschoolers with special needs* (2nd ed.). Boston, MD: Brookes.

Sanders, S. (2015). *Encouraging physical activity in infants*. Lewisville, NC: Gryphon House.

Snyder, C. (2016). Building intentional routines for infants and toddlers. *Highscope Extensions*, 30(2), 1–5.

Tamis-LeMonda, C. S., Kuchirko, Y., and Song, L. (2014). Why is infant language learning facilitated by parental responsiveness? *Current Directions in Psychological Sciences*, 23(2), 121–6.

Vernon-Feagans, L., Hurley, M. M., Yont, K. M., Wambolt, P. M., and Kolak, A. (2007). Quality of childcare and otitis media: Relationship to children's language during naturalistic interactions at 18, 24, and 36 months. *Journal of Applied Developmental Psychology*, 28, 115–33.

Weisleder, A., and Fernald, A. (2013). Talking to children matters: Early language experience strengthens processing and builds vocabulary. *Psychological Science*, 24(11), 2143–52.

About the Author

Dr. Sarah Taylor Vanover has been working in the field of early childhood for over eighteen years. She first began as an assistant teacher in an infant room, and since then she has served as a lead teacher, a program administrator, a trainer, and a classroom teaching coach. She has also had the opportunity to work at the state level to assist with policy development and supervise early childhood trainers throughout the Commonwealth of Kentucky. She is currently a professor of child development and family studies at Eastern Kentucky University, where she teaches courses on early childhood education and supervises student teachers.

Dr. Vanover completed her doctoral research on what families look for when selecting childcare for their children. She is an active trainer in Kentucky and surrounding states, and she frequently speaks at conferences on topics like quality childcare indicators, language development in the early childhood classroom, and the importance of quality infant and toddler care in early childhood education. For the past several years, she has focused her work and research on assessing quality early childhood programs for health and safety requirements and school readiness skills.

She lives in Lexington, Kentucky, with her husband, Rob, and their two sons, Jack and James.